Designing Your GARDEN

Marshall Cavendish

Contents

Published by
Marshall Cavendish Books Limited
58 Old Compton Street
London W1V 5PA

© Marshall Cavendish Limited 1972, 1973, 1974, 1975, 1976, 1977, 1978, 1979, 1980, 1981, 1982, 1983, 1984

Printed and bound in Italy
Grafiche Editoriali Padane, Cremona, Ita

ISBN 0 86307 320 4

Introduction

Whether you are the owner of a country estate, or merely the proud possessor of a window box, your garden is a part of your home.

With this book plus a little flair, you can turn your garden into a source of endless enjoyment, as well as actually increasing the value of your property. This picture-packed guide to garden design will give you all the expertise you need for a beautiful and well-planned garden. You can create a Japanese-style water garden, or launch into a large-scale landscaping project. If you enjoy home grown produce, incorporate a kitchen garden into an otherwise formal design.

Whatever your taste and however limited your garden facilities, here are some unusual ideas to add that special touch to your home, all beautifully illustrated in full colour.

Secrets of garden design

Garden planning is too often the 'poor relation' of home design. Many people consider landscaping the pursuit of only the very rich. But 'landscaping' is, after all, only another word for design. It could be as much a part of making your home more beautiful as a valuable work of art—only this time, you can do it for yourself.

Whether you are designing the garden of a new home or replanning an existing garden, restraint, balance and perspective are the laws that govern the master landscaper. You can lift even a small suburban garden out of the ordinary by coaxing natural materials and resources into symmetry.

Orientation

If, when you are buying a new house, you are lucky enough to have a choice of sites, consider the orientation or 'lie' of the plot. Think, for example, what parts of the garden will get reasonable amounts of sunlight, and which will fall in shade. In colder climates, a terrace which is shielded from the sun for most of the day by

the shadow of the house is virtually useless. Similarly, if you live in a country where shade is essential, plan for it from the outset. A garden which is too hot or too chilly to sit in at least during some months of the year is a wasted asset.

Many builders and developers construct areas of paving as part of their service. But check this on the plans—the terrace may be facing the wrong way, so that it would be continually enveloped in chilly shadows or blazing heat.

Access and site clearance

It may not seem to have a direct bearing on design, but the amount of rubbish and subsoil on the site, and the difficulty of access to the plot, may alter the total cost of garden construction drastically. Make sure, before they actually leave, that you understand what conditions the builders will leave behind. The cost of removing subsoil which has been dumped after foundation excavation can be

Top right. Unusual steps of spilling colour which soften the visual jump from level to level. The mossy old millstones provide interesting 'tubs' for the shrubs.
Bottom right. Tall, tendrilly plants frame a tapering path to welcome the visitor. The paving slabs are cut to provide a false perspective.

high, particularly if the access to the site has been restricted by fences or buildings. If part of the walling or fencing can be left open until the garden construction has been completed, a lot of time, and probably money, can be saved.

Services on new sites

While most builders and architects will agree to provide at least one external water tap and an electricity supply, it is not done automatically. Try to evolve a basic overall plan for the garden so that your builder or architect will know in advance, for example, whether you plan to have an electric pump or garden lighting. Also worth careful checking in the early stages is the siting of inspection covers. These often turn out to be just where you want to build a patio. This is not fatal, provided the covers are sited parallel to the joint lines of the patio paving. You can use a recessed cover to replace the standard metal cover, and conceal it under liftable slabs.

The lie of the land

Sloping ground can make a garden a great deal more interesting than can a completely flat site. In fact, with the exception of certain types of *formal* layout, landscaping on a flat site often begins with altering the levels to give more interest. The eye quickly gets bored with a flat horizon. Shapes and steps make for a livelier view. Land *rising* gently away from the house will mean that added features can be seen to better advantage. On the other hand, rising ground does tend to foreshorten the perspective and make even quite large gardens seem smaller.

Drainage can also be a problem in a garden which slopes towards the house. A drain line across the edge of the terrace will probably be called for, since the water running off the land will meet the water running off the terrace paving. If the drainage line is to end at a soak-hole, this should of course be placed as far as possible from the house.

Ground *sloping* away from the house, providing it falls gently, usually gives a feeling of spaciousness. It also adds depth to the perspective where there are wide views of surrounding gardens or the countryside. Special features in the garden itself may not always be visible from the house—but then, hidden features which one comes upon suddenly when exploring the garden are often a pleasant surprise.

Level sites

Though the heights of trees, shrubs and flowers can be 'stepped' to give the impression that the soil itself is at varying levels, a certain amount of grading is often needed to add an imaginative dimension to your garden. If the topsoil is thin, you will have to strip it off and respread it after grading the ground below. Grading to gentle flowing contours is particularly suited to informal gardens, which could successfully incorporate heathland and alpine meadowland effects. Providing the slopes are gentle and can be conveniently mown, the grass areas will look more mature.

Remember to grade lawns so that water cannot collect in depressions. If you want a 'dish', or concave effect in a grassed area, it is a good idea to site some planting or a rock outcrop at the lowest point to conceal a soakaway—or to use a pool, which looks most realistic in a depression. Soakaways under turf become visible in times of drought as the earth becomes dry and scorched where it is sharply drained.

Disposing of prunings and grass-cuttings can be a problem. Ugly incinerators, garden sheds, green-houses and cold frames can be concealed by careful planting, walls and fencing. The screening of frames or greenhouses can be tricky, as they need some light in order to function at all. Pierced screen walling or trelliswork is invaluable for this job.

Utility areas need hard paving around them, and an easy access path, which must be discreet or it will dominate the garden. You can make such a path more interesting if you lay it to gently curving lines, relying on planting or contouring the ground in front to break up the direct view. But do not forget that the favourite route to anywhere is usually the most direct and short cuts tend to be habit-forming. Nothing looks worse than trampled planting or battered grass near a pathway. You can literally 'get round' this by using tough plants, such as holly or gorse, which take the temptation out of short cuts!

Width of paths

The width of a path will be dictated by the total scale of the garden. This is the designer's rule, but gardens are primarily social places, so people must be considered, too. For two people to walk comfortably side by side, you will need a width of about 4ft, which is the absolute minimum. A path of less than 2ft in width will seem mean except in the tiniest gardens, and will be too awkward for manoeuvering barrows and mowers.

Patios and steps

It is pointless having a patio unless it is in perfect scale with the rest of the garden, and it is large enough to serve its purpose. A patio that extends less than 10ft in width will be far too restricted for any one to walk past fully extended deck chairs or a group of chairs and a table.

Unless a damp-proof course is incorporated into the terrace, the terrace should be 6in. below the house dpc line, which itself is often some 6in.-8in. below the floor level inside. Try not to make your step any deeper than this, or you will find it awkward and jolting.

Pattern for patios

Patios do not have to be rectangular. It is a good idea to break the hard line by introducing softer shapes or by using step features and plants. However, though curved lines are attractive, they are difficult to work to unless you use natural stone or crazy paving.

Some kind of a wall may be necessary to prevent small children falling from a raised terrace, in which case the best height is between 15in. and 18in. above the paving level. The wall will then 'double' as a seat for grown-ups. Walls that are too narrow, or 'dwarf', simply look ridiculous. If any kind of solid wall seems claustrophobic, you may prefer balustrading or using low screen walls coped to match the terrace paving. Hollow walls full of foliage help to soften what could be an unattractive, straight-edged line. Better still would be to leave an area for plants in front of the wall, where you could cultivate garden herbs. (This could be conveniently near the kitchen, perhaps.) Or you could plant 'pockets' in the paving with small herbs and other 'carpeting' plants.

The main steps down from a terrace or patio should be wide enough to accommodate several people at a party, or at least two people passing each other. Delicate steps look disproportionate, and can be dangerous. Line the steps up main windows, trying to get them the same width which will give you a clear and impressive view from inside the house. An informal alternative is 'L' shaped steps leading from one end of the patio into the garden.

The rise of *any* step should normally be between 4in. and 8in.—vary rarely more than this. The most comfortable tread width is between 9 and 18in. The step looks best if it overhangs the riser by 1in.—2in., which also helps deal with rainwater and creates an interesting shadow line.

Steps also need to follow a fairly definite set of proportions if they are to be comfortable and not awkward feeling. One formula is that the *going* (length of the step, not including any overhang) multiplied by the *rise* (height of the step) should be as close as possible to 66in.; the steeper the flight, the narrower the tread. So a step 6in. high should have a going of about 11in.

Remember that a mowing tread is essential at the base of steps and below terrace walls, where they meet the lawn. This is a line of paving or brick; in the case of steps, it can be the lowest tread, which should be set 1in. below the lawn level. This allows the mower to give a clean edge to the lawn and prevents it scuffing the masonry.

Creating vistas

If there is a view to distant countryside or to neighbouring trees, it will be worth designing the garden deliberately to 'frame' the view. This will naturally take the eye beyond the confines of your garden, adding to the effect of sweeping greenery. Do not despise features such as old trees and mossy tree-stumps, as they could be just the focal points your new garden may need. Established fruit trees, for example, if discreetly shaped and cleared of surrounding undergrowth so that the trees stand out by themselves, make good starting points. They can form the base for your whole landscape.

With an overgrown site, it is best to cut back gradually, removing the rubbish and diseased or decayed material first. Stand back from time to time and take a fresh look to see how the garden is taking shape. Hitherto unseen features will probably start emerging. Try not to clear *too* much—many potential assets have been lost by too-zestful grubbing and felling. However ordinary a tree may seem, it provides and 'authentic', unartificial look to your garden design.

Perspective

It is difficult to generalize on perspective, but there are certain basic rules which should always be obeyed.

Long narrow sites, particularly when bounded by wall, fence or hedge lines, should not be planted with straight borders which run parallel to the sides, or with long runs of continuous lawn. Straight paths running along the site may appear to converge in the distance like railway lines.

Borders which are informal in outline, and whose placement breaks up large expanses, help to minimize the 'canal towpath' look of long narrow garden.

Another important factor in perspective is the use of planting to emphasize or diminish the feeling of distance. If larged-leaved trees or bushes are used in the foreground, and the planting is graded to fine-leaved foliage in the background, the effect of distance is increased. This is heightened even more if the foreground plants are big themselves, not just bearing large leaves. The colour or foliage, too, plays an important part. Dense and dark green glossy foliage in the foreground, and silvery or blue-grey in the background, creates a hazy horizon looking further distant than it actually is.

For *too-wide sites,* most of the above advice should be reversed. In these gardens, long borders of relatively even width and paths running in the same line, will serve to extend the garden visually. It is even possible to cut stepping stones of a gradually decreasing size to give a false perspective, but you must be careful to scale plants and trees to match.

An extension to the house

Modern houses often have large ceiling-to-floor, clear-glazed windows which are a first starting point when linking the garden with the house. The 'through-view' establishes a flow

Below. High spot for hillside design! The formal sweep of grass away from the house adds a sense of space and dignity, and the planted area close up to the building flatters the white decor with its colour.

...bove. A formal layout benefits from the balance of colour and shape. The main area of ...wn is split up by groupings of flowers and ...es, so that wherever you look from the ...rden is a perfect blend of nature and art.

...m the garden to the sitting room or vice versa. ... wall which runs out from the house as an ...tension of one of the interior walls helps the ...tegration of house with garden, especially if ...e building materials are the same. If, like ...any houses today, one or more of your living ...om walls is of natural stone or raked brick-...ork, you can exploit this by following the ...aterials through as the new outer wall.

Paving can also be extended from the patio ...to the room itself. Even a single row of shrubs ...side sliding doors, or beside floor-to-ceiling ...indows, makes a noticeable improvement by ...ringing the garden into the room'. If you use ...rgola timbers above a patio, set them at the ...me height as the ceiling of the adjacent room. ...anting in the garden-room, particularly if ...irrored by plants immediately outside the glass, ...mpletes the integration of house and garden. ...hen planting inside the house, try to use plants ...hich are suited to both outside and inside ...owth, so that the same varieties can be ...anted on the patio or terrace.

...aths and utility areas

Gardens, much as we would like to imagine ...em otherwise, are not purely for recreation. It ... easy when in the throes of design, to forget ...at washing may be hung out regularly, and so ...rget to provide for washing lines or clothes ...yers. The modern clothes dryers which can be ...ut up when needed, simply slotting into a pre-cast socket are ideal. If possible, try to site them in paved areas where the housewife will not have to struggle across expanses of wet grass with heavy washing, and prevent the possibility of clothes blowing on to nearby planting. Some manufacturers provide a canopy with their dryers which makes an excellent sunshade—though of rather unwieldy proportions for the average suburban garden.

Rock and water in the garden

Water is always fascinating. Surrounded by rock and foliage it can be complex, mysterious and intriguing. Reflection and refraction add colour and depth to a garden. Water naturally provides optical illusions rather like mirrors.

But remember that garden pools are notorious hazards for small children. They may *look* innocently shallow, but they are responsible for many deaths a year. Bearing this in mind it may be worth foregoing the actual water in the pool until children are old enough to enjoy it safely; in the meantime, you could consider constructing the basin and fitting it up with all the plumbing, provision for a pump and so on. Then you can seal off the connections and fill the basin with silver sand to make an excellent sandpit. Another idea is to introduce water in the form of a spring or 'gusher', with the water bubbling up from a bed of pebble and boulder, which conceals the pool basin. There will then be no large area of water for curious toddlers to fall into.

Siting the water

If you plan to use rock and water in a natural setting, remember to site it clear of trees with a large leaf fall which could foul the surface, and

Top right. Step-by-step garden design! A courtyard elegance created by gravel, concrete and water. The success of the design lies in its absolute simplicity; lifting shallow water up to the sun provides sparkle, and the leafy surrounds soften the line.
Bottom right. A pool rimmed with paving and flanked with old stone looks natural, but only artificial pools reach those heights! Masses of brilliant blooms flatter the fine old walling, but the shrubs are banked up to soften the hard grey stone.

away from heavy shade which ruins the potential beauty.

Do not try to fight the natural 'lie' of the water. Trying to lift a water-and-rock feature would simply look wrong. Even when the ground slopes away from the house, it is better to accept that the pool will have to be viewed from further down the garden. A mere glimpse of water falling from a rock face is enough to invite closer appreciation.

Rock sizes

Massive-scale rockwork is not for small gardens, unless you want to dwarf the whole neighbourhood. On the other hand, many gardeners go to the other extreme, using tiny bits of stone which only create a 'toy' garden impression. If you are to recreate the sort of strata and outcrops found in nature, it is impossible to do so with tiny stones, because they have little natural 'bed' or strata themselves. Unless you are prepared to shift stones of $\frac{1}{2}$cwt to 3cwt, it is better to think in terms of the pebble-and-boulder groupings associated naturally with lowland streams.

Get a lot from your plot

The average British suburban garden is just a strip of land behind a 'semi'. In this context, the very word 'landscaping', with its connotations of stately homes and parks, may seem laughable. But skilful landscaping, adapted to the ordinary family garden, can camouflage its drawbacks and enormously expand its appeal.

What do you want from your garden? Most people would describe a garden as, ideally, a place to relax, a place that is beautiful to look at, preferably the whole year round . . . and a place that is easy to keep that way. A few people do make a fetish out of gardening and are happiest when weeding or mowing, but even for such hobbyists landscaping can make life easier. Landscaping means *planning*, and planning means efficiency—so that your garden can be easily kept in good order, and just as easily developed and improved.

The paved garden

If you are not one of nature's fanatical gardeners, then a paved garden may suit you best. Natural stone walling goes well with paved ground, so you could take advantage of this and have absolute privacy and old-world charm at the same time. Climbing plants can usually be coerced into decorating at least one wall, their greenery contrasting harmoniously with the mellow tones of natural materials. With most of the ground space paved, maintenance is down to the absolute minimum of sweeping, and weeding between the slabs. The danger, though, is creating a monastery-like, cloistered feeling, and brightly coloured shrubs should be encouraged to flourish in such surroundings, if only in tubs. Small established trees which have grown near a mossy wall may be yours already, if your house is old. Leave this composite picture as it is—it could not be bettered by the best landscape gardener.

Rose gardens

Average-sized gardens that aim for the 'English country garden look' often end up a blaze of colour in season—and a tangle of tawdry thornbushes out of season. Smallish gardens will always benefit from both colour and a fair measure of magnificence, but the amateur garden-planner is all too often carried away by the promises of rose-growers' brochures, which *do* 'flower' all year round.

If you cannot afford space for a whole garden that will be lifeless for much of the year, try growing your roses in isolated 'islands' in a paved area. Thus presented in single clumps or bushes, they will invite closer appreciation. Alternatively, grow roses in mixed shrub borders, or simply instead of shrubs.

If you do have the space, though, roses are *the* flowers for any formal layout. They are set off well by dark green evergreen foliage, and the traditional conifer hedges, especially yew,

are still probably the most effective back ground. If you plan such a feature, remembe when planting that you are going to nee reasonable space between the mature ros bushes and the face of a mature hedge whicl you will have to clip into shape.

Whatever the shapes of the rose beds you ar planning, it is better to work them out to scal first on squared paper. Try to keep the design a simple as possible—and avoid trying to cram i too many varieties of bloom. The temptation i to have variety at all cost—sometimes at th cost of good looks. One way out is to have on bed, the central one for example, as a cut flower area of mixed varieties, and to plant th surrounding bed area with massed groups o single varieties. Better still, grow all the roses herbaceous, foliage and annual plants fo cutting in an out-of-the-way site in an odc corner of the garden. This will take the eye tc

Below, left. *A balanced-life pond adds a cool note to this summer garden. Flowering shrubs are clustered round it to invite closer inspection and appreciation.*

Below, right. *Climbing plants and roses camouflage the high brick walls of this town garden. Paving stones are subtly laid between patches of grass and colourful plants.*

e unexpected corner, thus 'filling out' the
arden visually and making it seem larger than
is.

The point about planning, incidentally,
pplies also to every other feature. Drawn to
cale before you begin to build or knock down,
e future garden can be envisaged more easily
nd alterations made, if necessary, before it is
o late. Mistakes involving walling or paving,
or example, can be very expensive.

tepping out of line

Attempts to landscape the average garden
ften lead to too much regimentation—square
lots of lawn, and long strips of paving leading
o a starkly rectangular garden. Modern
rchitecture, including 'typical' council houses
1 Britain, only too often seems to fall in with
is feeling that everything *has* to follow a
eometrical pattern. In rare cases, a modern

house can be flattered by a purely formal garden
and surrounds, but this usually works only for
the very large garden or the naturally skilled
landscaper.

Most gardens have a square or rectangular
shape, set off only by the neighbour's fencing or
your own hedge. It may not take much, however—even for the lazy gardener—to change
the shape of the garden, or at least its apparent
shape. A clump of shrubs off-centre, a diagonal
path, or a pool at the bottom of your garden
would all add interest—and make you feel
much less like a pawn on a chessboard.

Even in a fairly small area, a change of levels
can give the eye extra dimensions to enjoy. You
can define different parts of your garden by, for
example, moving a few inches of topsoil from
one part of the plot to another, and planting
unusually shaped or unusually coloured plants
on the raised part. Basically, it is the same idea

*Above. A perfect setting for a simple
rose garden—just one variety of blooms in
a circular bed with walk-around paving.
The greenery sets off the pink tones.*

as the tried and tested rockery.

If you are going to have a pool, it is better to
leave the rockery to surround that than to
overdo it and clutter up your garden with too
many rocks.

Trees are invaluable as aids for optical
illusion. They automatically carry the eye sky-
wards. Think hard before cutting a tree;
natural features are easily destroyed, but slow
to replace.

Pools and the use of water

If your garden is large enough to 'take' a
moderate-sized pool, then take advantage of it
—it could be one of your greatest assets. A

7

Above, main picture. *A slate rockery banked up on either side of a winding path; its greyness offset with mosses, ferns and shrubs in toning colours and rounded shapes.*
Above, inset. *One section of an English cottage garden reserved for colour. Slabs of irregularly shaped rock form stepping stones among the rockery plants.*

largish area of still water, reflecting trees or simply the sky, is an unparalleled source of interest, and not only for the very young. As opposed to playpools, 'natural' pools can have, literally, a life of their own. Water plants, fish, insects, algae—and mud—are all necessary for a 'balanced life' pond. After the initial installation they will look after themselves.

Apart from clearing off leaves and other 'foreign' debris, do not make the mistake of trying to clean out one of these 'nature' pools. Nature simply will not be cleaned out. Pond plants oxygenate the water, water snails and other pond creatures constantly clean it. The mud will settle after a few weeks, providing a bed for plants and other pond life; if the pool is properly balanced, it will stay clean and healthy.

A stagnant pool without life will attract dirt and grow slimy very quickly. There are no short cuts—if you want a pretty, clear, tiled pool where you can always see the bottom, you will have to clean it out thoroughly and often. This means scrubbing the tiles and changing the water.

A 'natural' pond, complete with life, needs enough depth for that life to flourish and find shade—down to 3ft. Any deeper, and the sun-

light cannot penetrate sufficiently to keep th plants oxygenated and the reflections cease be interesting, only confused. Try to site yo pond where there will be enough sun, at lea for some of the year. Stagnant ponds continua in shade breed unhealthiness and are gloomy look at.

A marginal area of 'aquatic' planting rour the pool will draw attention to it, but if th plants are allowed to enclose the pool entire then they ruin the effect by shutting it off fro view and looking unnatural.

Natural pools will be sited at the lowe point of the garden; otherwise they cease to natural. Water finds its own level, and that never up! Formal—more artificial—pools ca have the land re-graded to accommodate ther but most gardens simply lack the land to r

PICTUREPOINT

HARRY SMITH

ade in the first place.

If you have a choice, avoid siting your pool der a tree with a heavy leaf-fall. Trees create autiful reflections, but a large accumulation leaf and plant debris will quickly silt up slow stagnant water and turn it foul.

amouflage and perspective

Few gardens that 'come with the house' are al shapes. But you can make them seem ger, for example, through the cunning use of aded paving. Everyone knows about perective—that lines seem to converge at the rizon, even though they remain the same stance apart when you are actually walking tween them. With a bit of thought, you can e this rule to make a squat, box-shaped rden look a longer, more elegant shape.

Above, main picture. A formal layout for a split-level garden. The greens of hedge, trees and lawn blend perfectly with the greys of the wall and steps.
Above, inset. A neat, bright driveway, kept immaculately and geometrical in form. The diamond-shaped flower bed complements both curving and straight walls.

Simply grade the width of each paving stone so that the last one (the one furthest away) is the narrowest. It plays exactly the right trick on your eye—the garden seems yards longer. The reverse applies to absurdly long, thin gardens. Put the narrowest stone nearest to you, the widest at the end of the path. The end will then be in sight!

Alternately, use the same rules for shortening,

or lengthening that you would use to camouflage a room's dimensions, stressing the horizontal lines to shorten, vertical to lengthen.

Essentially simple

A regimented-looking garden is bad, but an over-complicated, fussy plot is worse—an insult to the good materials you have to hand. The Japanese are masters of the art of landscaping; to them it is a serious study. You may not want one of their stylized, oversimplified gardens, but they do teach one lesson: a few well-chosen plants, the glitter of water and the curve of a branch become things of breathtaking beauty when used together in their practised hands. In short, the simpler the scheme, the more effective it is likely to be, and the easier to keep that way.

Making more of a mini-garden

In towns, the word 'garden' is often misleading. Often the American term 'yard' would be more descriptive. Plenty of town back gardens are merely small square or rectangular patches between two rows of back-to-back terrace houses—each one, probably, with a frontage of no more than 15ft. Sometimes, too, such a garden is found in the central well formed by an extension or as an integral part of an architect-designed complex of new housing.

These mini-gardens need treating in quite a different way from larger ones. For a start, paving almost always looks better than grass in a confined space. (A combination of children and wet grass can result, anyway, in a sea of mud in no time at all.) A scaled-down version of the conventional herbaceous border planted down one side looks not only boring but cramped. And left completely alone, such a backyard is nothing but an eyesore—especially when seen through living room or dining room windows.

Garden walls

Almost always, a tiny garden is enclosed; a one or two of its walls may be formed by t back or sides of another house.

This enclosure is often an advantage. Hi walls shut off noise, besides giving privacy plus a lot more gardening space. But as t brickwork will be seen when the last leaf h fallen from the last creeper, it is important th walls are treated as an integral part of t garden itself.

If you wish to extend your walling, wov wooden palings (which need creosoting protect them from the weather) are compar tively cheap, but not particularly versatile. good brick wall is much more satisfactory. many places, too, the heights of side walls, a the materials in which they may be built, a limited by local authority regulations; firepro materials are often preferred, or compulsor when a wall is on a boundary.

Brick walls, provided they are in good repa can be colourwashed in any of the pale, prett sugar-almond colours that are almost as ligh reflecting as white. Although white itself is fres

Opposite left. A tiny back garden made a maze of colour by a terrace banked high with bright shrubs and greenery at different levels.
Top, this page. A small yard livened up by introducing both paved and grassed areas surrounded by bright white walls.
Below, this page. A sophisticated angle for a corner garden! The goldfish pool adds a cool note to the paved outside lounge.
Right. Using the subtle shades of green against moss and mellow stone. The light shines attractively through the foliage.

and gay, it goes dirty extremely quickly; and on a grey winter's day looks cold and depressing. The hint-of-a-tint given by the admixture of pink, ochre, or turquoise—even a cupful or two to the gallon makes a difference—to the basic white paint gives a warmer, slightly 'Mediterranean' look. In warmer, crisper climates, white walls or palings look brilliant in sunlight.

This Mediterranean look can be backed up by using pretty bits of ceramics or glass—for instance, lining an alcove in the wall with tiny, brilliant blue Italian glass mosaic tiles. Then there are small, fairly cheap, weatherproof ceramic ones that could cover a projecting ledge to make a plant table. Even an unpromising basement area wall can be prettied up by painting it a light, gay colour and hanging a few random Portuguese or Spanish patterned tiles.

A piece of mirror in the garden is another simple but effective idea. Try a tall one to reflect a narrow little cypress tree, or a squarer one angled behind an urn full of spilling geraniums. A generous slab of mirror on a wall behind a wide-spaced trellis supporting a tangle of blue morning glories, for example, can appear to add yards of beauty to a tiny garden. Be careful, though, to use mirror just far enough from a cultivated area that the rain cannot splash it with mud streaks.

Levels

In a tiny garden, you should 'think vertically' as well as 'thinking horizontally'. In other words, it is important to create a series of points of interest at different heights.

If you want to pack the garden with plants and flowers, this means aiming for the effect of standing in the middle of a flower basket, with a lot of blooms at eye or shoulder level, rather than looking down on flat, ground-level beds, such as you might use in a larger garden.

Achieving different flowerbed levels usually means a lot of hard work at first. Topsoil must be carefully removed. A foundation of rubble, gravel, or builders' debris must be built up and shaped into a miniature landscape of hills and valleys, then the topsoil replaced over this foundation. As there will now be a greater surface area to cover, more topsoil must either be bought, or brought up sack by sack from the country. (Most town topsoil is stale; so take advantage of this preparing stage to add whatever is needed, from moisture-retaining peat to fertilizer.)

Once the beds are made, they can be broken up into small separate areas by brickwork, or paths made from flagstone pieces. These paths are not just decorative: they provide firm squatting-stones when you want to plant or weed. Lilliputian terraces, like small fields or vineyards descending a hill, can be equally effective, especially with hanging or trailing

plants. Brick edging can be used here, or dry stone walling made from pieces of flat stone, or paving chips too small for any other use.

A corner for leisure

If you prefer to devote the whole of a tiny garden to a flat space for children's play, sitting about, or sunbathing, it becomes even more important to concentrate a lot of the interest higher than the basic ground level to avoid a 'walled-up' feeling. Should you be lucky enough to have a tree growing in one corner of the garden, you have a ready-made solution; if not, you could plant your own tree; concentrate on climbing plants—perhaps growing a vine or wisteria right up the side of the house; fix pots to the walls; or site plant boxes on the top of walls to trail foliage downwards.

Materials

A plain sweep of lawn looks magnificent in the open spaces of a large garden; in a tiny one, a certain amount of cunning and intricacy works best. Even the Japanese, masters of the simple, single-spray-in-a-vase school of flower arranging, avoid this approach in their tiny gardens; each one is a balanced, but complicated, little masterpiece.

In a paved garden, try a few contrasting materials. A sunburst of bricks around a tree, a miniature patio area near the house, covered in leather-brown quarry tiles, or old-fashioned cobblestones to outline or emphasize the paving itself, add a richness to an otherwise boring area.

In Britain, beautiful old paving stones with varying grey-gold colours and slightly irregular surfaces can be bought cheaply (especially if broken or damaged) from local councils who are replacing pavement surfaces. Almost anywhere, you can find mellow old bricks from a house that is being demolished or converted. Although this material can be chipped or broken, and sometimes needs hours of work to strike off old mortar, its textured surface or matured colouring are much more attractive than the flat regularity of cement or concrete paving.

In a paved garden, allowance should always be made for drainage. You can arrange this by making a very slight slope towards a central drainage hole or small grid, or towards several cracks between paving stones which are not cemented together, but loose-filled with gravel or sand.

Providing a focus

All tiny gardens need some kind of focus—if only to remove the impression of standing in a small square box. Trees, water, plants, statuary, all (though not all together!) make good focal points.

A focal point tree, should be the sort that is a good shape even when the branches are bare, or should be an evergreen.

Views vary on the use of water in gardens. Streams and small lakes are one thing; small stagnant-looking pools covered with a floating debris of leaves and insects are another. Part of the charm of any garden is movement (think of swaying branches, bird flight) so that running water is always a delight—the sunlit fountains in the stone courtyards of Spanish houses are perfect examples. Fountains may be beyond our reach, but a birdbath is within reach of all—perhaps an old stone one, perhaps a new but weathered-looking fibreglass one, placed on the edge of a banked-up terrace bed. Plant a small shrub, some ferns, or a few small, bright flowers nearby, and you almost have the effect of a miniature pool.

Statuary, which can mean anything from an exquisite small bronze to a stone urn, heightens interest in any garden. Few people can afford really superb pieces—but anyone who can afford to consider a piece of sculpture might reflect that it is often seen at its best out of doors.

There are, too, all sorts of smaller items that enhance a small space, from a sundial bought when an old house is demolished to a modern fibreglass urn whose shape and pattern are taken from an eighteenth century mould. Large terracotta flowerpots, in different shapes and sizes, are particularly flattering—and are cheap. Even a clutch of chimneypots or drainpipes, of different widths and heights, grouped together and planted with ivy or geraniums, can make a decorative and interesting focal point.

Plants

Focal-point plants should have a very definite shape. The stiffness of a large yucca, the dark formality of a little cypress, are good examples. Remember that pencil-shaped trees, such as flowering cherries, block out less light from the rest of the garden. The sort with angular bare branches, like figs or magnolias, let light through in a dappled pattern, as well as providing interesting shapes.

Although what can be planted in a garden depends to a large extent on the type of soil, climate, rainfall, and so forth, successful planting of a small garden depends on certain other factors as well.

As most very small gardens are in towns, with high walls surrounding them, they usually get very little light indeed. This means using plants that thrive in dark conditions. This, in turn, means depending on greenery rather than blooms.

Space is usually so limited that bare earth looks much more desolate than in a larger garden. Coat flowerbeds between plants and shrubs with tiny, quick-spreading ground-level green plants; this will also stop weeds growing.

In a mini-garden, each plant is an individual. A permanent one must pay its way in terms of shape or foliage for most of the year, if it is not to leave a gap like an extracted tooth when flowering time is over. Others may be best planted singly, or sparingly, otherwise their effect may be to pull the rest of the garden out of scale, when they are not in bloom. In a tiny area, three yellow crocuses give just as much of an effect of spring as an orchardful in a country garden. For brilliant colour, or scent, a few bedding-out plants or seedlings can be installed in chosen sites, in tubs or urns.

Lighting

One of the advantages of a tiny garden is that it can so easily be floodlit. Just one lamp, tucked beneath the house window, and beaming on to the plants opposite, may be all that is needed. Or it could be set at ground level behind a statue, to throw this and the surrounding shrubs into relief; or spiked into a flowerbed to illuminate some particularly decorative bloom.

The dramatic effect of the interplay of light and shadows in a small, lit-up garden creates a living picture-wall for anyone indoors in the dining or sitting room. It is especially effective if you are entertaining—and is, incidentally, a burglar-deterrent.

For outdoor lighting, always use the correct, specially-designed, outdoor plugs and sockets, for safety's sake.

An extra room?

If you are short of living space, you may wish to treat a small back garden primarily as an extra living room, or as an extension of a kitchen-dining room, especially in warm weather. In this case a glazed (or better still, double-glazed) door into the garden gives a sense of extra space and continuity where a conventional wooden door would act as a view-stopper.

Sometimes it is possible to use flooring to add to this sense of continuity. Quarry tiles on the kitchen floor can be continued outside to form a small patio, and possibly link up with cobbles and brickwork to make a patterned garden 'floor'.

The mini-garden that is used as a 'room' has to provide several of the functions of a real room. Warmth, privacy and shelter can be given by high walls or palings. For a verandah effect, cover a third or half the garden with a pergola or some other roof structure. This can be glazed, fitted with pull-down slatted wooden or canvas sunblinds, or twined with climbing plants.

If there is sufficient shelter, outdoor cooking may be possible. This could be on a brick barbecue built along one wall, or on a simple brick or tiled counter top fitted with outlet sockets for various plug-in appliances. (Remember to use special outdoor plugs and sockets).

In an extra 'room' of this kind, seating is important. Mini-gardens often belong to small-ish houses so that, while there is plenty of attractive garden furniture available, finding somewhere to store it is a problem. An alternative to the white-painted iron seat, or teak bench, that can be left out all year round, is built-in seating. A brick or concrete block bench down the length of one wall can be softened with a scatter of gingham cushions for impromptu outdoor meals, and double as a parking place for glasses if you have a small drinks party—or even, since your outdoor room is still a garden, as a table for plant pots!

Landscaping for the awkward plot

Most sites present some problems to the amateur landscaper, but there are some which seem impossible to deal with. They may be peculiar shapes or sizes, where conventional paving and planting look wrong, no matter how they are juggled around. And often, what makes a site interesting is also its undoing. A site overlooking the sea, for example, may be your romantic ideal—but what will grow under all that salt-spray and wind?

No matter where you live, however, nature will have found some plants which suit your particular type of soil. It is just a question of finding out what they are, and if horticulture has produced any refinements. Usually, too, a few simple devices employed in a strangely-shaped garden can make you the proud owner of something highly-personalized, a garden which is impossible to copy, though easy to envy!

Difficult soils

There are few soil-types which will refuse to support some form of plant life. So before you despair of your barren patch and start a costly process of importing soil, try to list all the possible plants likely to survive on your site. With some help from your local nurseryman, the list will turn out longer than you envisaged. He

will of course be raising plants tolerant of your type of soil, so before you start ordering from far away, where plants may be raised on a totally different soil, ask his advice.

It is a good idea, too, to find out what wild plants thrive in your area; many cultivars will be descended from them, and a comparison between the local flora and the nurseryman's catalogue can be very revealing. Take heather,

for example. If it grows in abundance locall[y] your nurseryman may offer a tremendous rang[e] of cultivated varieties, with differing colou[r] foliage and flowering periods.

Exposed sites

On exposed ground, particularly near coast[al] areas, you may need to shelter choice plant[s] from the prevailing wind by using tough[er] varieties as a screen. A typical screen coul[d] comprise a tree-line, often conifer, to act as [a] wind-break, and then a graded planting [of] shrubs tolerant of salty soil. Once this screen [is] established, you may well find that the soil ca[n] support 'foreign' plants not generally found i[n] the area because of their aversion to salt an[d] wind.

But remember that it will take time for thi[s] screen planting to be successful. Each part o[f] the screen will have to reach a stage where [it] affords protection to the next less toleran[t] plants, and so on, gradually setting up an almos[t] total protection. It is also true that such plantin[g] can obstruct the view seawards—often th[e] main reason for choosing the site in the firs[t] place! If no compromise is possible, an alterna[-] tive is simply to complement the existing land[-] scape with a few of the trees and grasses nativ[e] to the area, relying on a rock group or larg[e] pieces of driftwood to add interest and creat[e] focal points. In this way, integration with th[e] natural surroundings is practically done for you[.] And it is always effective.

Steep slopes

Extreme gradients are often too costly t[o] terrace and difficult to maintain. They can[,] however, be planted with 'tumbledown', o[r] cascade-effect planting or with rambling an[d] climbing plants. Many of these plants, particu[-]

__Below.__ A triangular site packed with well-proportioned features. The round lawn 'takes the edges' off the look of the site.

y self-clinging climbers, normally used on
lls or fences, will quickly cover sharply rising
und. Those plants which re-root from
ling stems are especially useful, as they will
p hold the soil and stop it washing away.
cause of the sharp drainage on acutely
gled slopes, the plants will need to be fixed
o pockets cut into the slope and big enough
hold water at least until the plants are
ablished. Ground cover plants are not so good
steep slopes—you need more of them, and it
es more work to get them established.
sides, they do not prevent the possibility of a
l slip, and may even aggravate erosion.

ardens with odd corners

Sites which run to acutely angled corners,
ngular sites in particular, present something
a problem. If the main viewpoint is directed
o the apex of a triangle, it gives a sense of
se perspective. For this reason, formal hedges
beds running parallel to the angles of the
ex should be avoided. If you want a lawn on
ur triangular site, it is best to make it circular,
us softening the harsh angularity of the plot.
circle is usually the most easily mown in such
ses, and does give a reasonable amount of
vn.

aking use of corners

Acute-angled corners, particularly where
ice or wall lines meet, need careful planting if
u need to mask them. A standard tree or
nifer planted close into the corner will help a
eat deal in relieving the sharp edge. But before
essing up' these corners, think what utility

SAM LAMBERT

Above. *A backyard made beautiful! This dim corner is landscaped for visual impact. Gentle rises covered in ground-hugging moss, and tall shrubs give the feeling of space.*

Below. *The harsh angularity of this site is softened by the wavy contours of the lawn, and curved areas of shrubs. The paved corner makes for a cosy and sheltered viewpoint.*

DON KIDMAN

areas you may need. Compost heaps, sheds—and practical plots such as salad or herb gardens—can be fitted neatly into these difficult patches. Generally speaking, it is better to stick to a layout which is primarily composed of informal flowing curves. Or, if it must be formal, base it on a circular design. Any attempt to introduce straight paths or rectangular borders will only emphasize the eccentricity of your garden.

Using corners for seats

If an acute-angled corner has a favourable aspect with a reasonable view, it will often make a cosy private place for a seat. The lines of walls, fences or planting converging at that point will give it a feeling of importance, rather like being at the hub of a wheel. And as you relax in such a spot, the diverging lines opening out in front of you create a spacious, luxurious feeling.

Paving into corners

If you are using crazy paving, you will have few problems running it into tight corners. But if you are using the more conventional rectangular paving, you will probably want to avoid even trying to negotiate the corners. Try using pebble or cobble setts instead, but not on the outer edge of any raised area, where they might kick out and break away.

Plants and containers

An internal angle on a terrace, especially a windy one, will always accumulate dust and debris. Certain types of plants are ideal for such corners, which are often also shady and damp. Though litter of any size will still have to be removed by hand, such plants will conceal dust and fallen leaves, gradually building up new foliage over them. Ferns, in particular are well suited to this 'job'; so are evergreen carpeting, and climbing plants like hedera.

Plants in tubs also help to conceal or camouflage corners or odd angles. A wide range of pots, urns, and modern ceramic or fibreglass

Above. A pleasant corner of a patio with interesting effects of light and shade. Tubs of leafy shrubs and climbing plants set off different types of brickwork and paving.

Below. Paving into corners can be a tough job especially with conventional slabs. Here cobble setts are used tight up to the wall, with the main terrace in tinted stone.

ontainers are available. Set full or tall plants at
le back of the container, with lower or
ascading plants at the front to soften the effect.
his will draw the eye away from any claustro-
hobically high walls.

Using mirrors

Long, narrow sites, or sites with a greatly
reshortened perspective, can sometimes be
orrected and improved by the use of mirrors!
here are a number of mirrored materials on the
narket, mirror board and tiles and it is even
ossible to mount the flexible plastic types on
 curved surface, though there will be some
istortion.

Mirrors need careful planning, however. If
ou have a site where the rear wall is too close to
le house, patio or main viewing point,
rategically placed mirrors can have spectacular
ffect—if they are not overdone. Multiple
nages formed by adjacent mirrors set at an
ngle to one another can be very disconcerting,
 too great an area is backed with mirror. For
xample, multiple images of your favourite
owering shrub may be pleasing, but frag-
nented images of people admiring it may have a
ightmarish quality! Boulders, sculptures, or
milar three-dimensional subjects placed close
 a mirror can result in strange back-to-back
ews, as though there were two identical pieces.

If you are thinking of using plant containers in
 mirrored scheme, consider using fibreglass
nes which can be cut in half vertically and, with
le backs 'made good' with sheet material,
laced against a mirror. The result can be very
ramatic. Probably the best use of a mirror in the
arden is where it backs mixed and massed
lanting, since the plants serve to break the
eflected image. Trellis, closely applied to the
nirror surface, is probably the best way of
xtending the visual line of climbing and flower-
ng plants, especially if the climbers are pruned
 geometric patterns. Often, fragmented
nages of flowers are more spectacular than one
ngle reflected clump.

Above. An unusual basement garden which
is created entirely with chips of stone as
an unconventional 'floor covering', and a
few potted palms as cool greenery.

Below. Dramatic use of mirror for a very
foreshortened perspective. The reflection
completes the image of the half-pool, and
the flowering border flanks it attractively.

Above. *A larger garden allows you to experiment with a number of 'special effects'. This pleasant glade looks like part of a natural forest.* *Left.* *Dartington Hall, Totnes, Devon, landscaping at its best.*

Large-scale landscaping without being outlandish

f your garden is so large that it almost herits the term 'park', you could be the wner of an impressive sweep of land, large area of countryside which is a lace of beauty to be envied. On the other hand, you could find yourself embedded in surroundings of unpararelled disorder. The scope is there for inspiration, but the room is also there for problems.

A large garden can fulfil many functions, apart from the usual ones of strolling and sunbathing. With room to spare, you can plan for recreation areas such as tennis courts or a children's playground. Or, on a more formal note, you can use elaborate water displays such as a series of fountains. Or you can try miniature parkland effects such as alpine planting. But considerable maintenance is involved with many of these ideas—and trying to incorporate them all can result in an unattractive, unwieldly mess.

Elegant grassland

A simple, and often elegant, way of land-scaping large areas is to create a 'parkland' or 'miniature parkland' effect. In these, the accent is on expanses of grass, with groupings of trees and the larger sorts of shrubs. Rather than including a formally arranged orchard, this method can make good use of groups of standard or bush fruit trees, mixed with ornamental flowering trees and shrubs.

The easiest things to control over large areas are grass, paving, ground cover, and trees. Of these, grass areas are usually by far the most economical to maintain. This is particularly true of 'rough grass'. Apart from a plot of closely mown grass near the house itself, the rest of the grassland can be rough grass undersown with bulbs. The bulbs will often surround groups of trees, which could be linked by paths of close-mown grass. The shapes of these areas should follow easy curves, to make mowing easier. The beauty of 'rough grass' is that where it is too inconvenient to mow, you can simply ignore it and let it grow.

Ground cover

Apart from grassing large areas, another useful way of reducing maintenance is to use ground cover planting. Its aim is to cover the area as quickly and densely as possible, thus allowing little competition from weeds. By their very nature, such plants, which fight for space, are not ideal for mixing with more 'choice' planting which they may choke and stunt in growth. Maintenance will be easier if such planting is restricted by surrounds of close-mown grass or hard paving.

The ground cover plants will need trimming to even up their shape from time to time, and feeding periodically because they tend to use up natural nutrients rapidly and may start to die. It is best not to mix types of ground cover plants. The usual approach is to mass plants in groups (you can take advantage of the cheap rates offered by nurserymen for bulk purchases). Ground cover is particularly useful in areas of deep shade, where grass would get thin and patchy, and where hard paving would become slippery and mossy.

Pools for larger gardens

Larger gardens, obviously, can 'take' more elaborate pool systems than small gardens can. While some basic principles remain the same there may be drainage problems and formal pools require separate consideration.

An enclosed rose or herb garden, or her-baceous border, can greatly enhance a lily pool or pools. The outline of the pool will often echo the general outline of the surrounding site, with other paths and beds radiating from, or parallel to, its lines. Here is an excellent place to site your fountain. The stillness of an enclosed area amplifies the sound of the most modest fountain—an effect often lost on an open site.

Except in rare cases, it is a mistake to try to include fountains in 'natural' water schemes. Fountains, after all, are not natural phenomena, and the fussy display of a 'jet set' in the terminal pool of a natural watercourse can ruin an other-wise harmonious effect. If you plan to use water-lilies in the pool, remember that the heavy

movement and splash from a fountain will not be tolerated by many plants.

A formal pool in an open, paved area is a popular feature. If the area immediately beyond the terrace is informal in design, you will find a circular pool less 'obvious' and jarring than a rectangular one.

On an exposed site, you may have problems if you use a fountain with too fine a jet spray. It may be wind-blown to the extent that it is pointless to have a fountain at all. Loss of water can seriously endanger any pumping equipment, so you need a mains compensatory system to top up the water.

If there are a series of pools, connect the higher ones to the lower by valved drainage lines. The main pool should have a sump and drain at its lowest point; it is usual to include an overflow pipe connected to the main drains to carry away excess rainwater. This, and occasionally flooding the pools deliberately, helps to keep the surface clean. The overflow pipe can be removed if you want to drain the whole system. The sump need not be out in the middle of the pool—no-one likes to wade out to remove a blockage or clean filters or skimmer units. So plan to have the low point easily accessible.

If you are planning a natural rock stream, you may be tempted to line up all the waterfalls so they can be seen together. But in nature, while the falls lie in line with the rock stratum generally, they are seldom straight for any distance. So alter the angles, and conceal some of the falls from direct view to achieve a more natural look. Your scheme will be more attractive if you can see only part of it from any given viewpoint. It will invite the visitor closer, since the sound of falling water is always an enticement anyway.

Herb gardens

It is sensible to site herb gardens near the house, handy to the kitchen. Most herbs are suitable for paved areas, and you can achieve very pleasing patterns by clumping them in the paving design. The different colours of purple sage, lavender, lemon thyme and parsley, for instance, form an attractive small garden by themselves. Another advantage is that certain herbs, the mints in particular, are difficult to control in open ground because of their excessive root action, but where they are isolated in paving they present no such problem.

Top left. A dignified old-world terrace enhanced by the skilful use of mosses and flowering shrubs planted between slabs of crazy paving. Steps lead up from this area to a raised lawn with a colourful border.
Top right. The formal lines of paths and a square lily pond are offset by the delicate shapes and tones of the surrounding plants. Roses and irises add spots of colour.
Below left. An old brick archway used to frame a view of lawn and evergreens. Cobblestones, red brick and a large stone urn are set against the variegated greenery.
Below right. Japanese-style design for a Western garden. The extreme simplicity of the immaculate lawn and stony stream-bed is garden design at its most effective.

ERIC LYONS ARCHITECT/SPAN DEVELOPMENTS LTD.

Wild gardens

The complete contrast to the formally laid-out garden is the 'wild' garden. This is not necessarily just acres of ground running happily to seed. A certain amount of planning and maintenance is involved, though pruning or weeding is, by definition, minimized in such a scheme. Some weeds can be allowed to grow, though the 'legitimate' plants must be dominant enough to be unaffected by the competing weeds.

An example of this is an area where there is a natural swamp or dew pond. This will have the usual collection of sedges, rushes, ferns and so on—and by adding a collection of plants and shrubs compatible in nature and which thrive in these conditions, you can achieve a most natural and attractive effect. Often, such areas include old tree stumps which would best be left alone, adding to the 'wild' effect.

If you plan a wild garden, try to keep other plantings apart; otherwise the natural weeds and grasses will seed themselves in the more formal areas. For this reason, wild garden areas are often associated with woodland glades, or set in the low parts of large lawns or rough grass areas.

Top left. A clean-cut and fresh-looking front driveway. The lawn is raised round the edges to give a 'dish' effect, and the base of the nearside tree is surrounded with a square of ground-cover planting.
Below left. A quiet island of graceful greenery set in a concrete drive. There is provision for night-time floodlighting.

Paving for the larger garden

Apart from the paving of patios and access paths, large areas of hard paving will reduce maintenance to a large extent. Brick and stone paving is expensive; instead, you might consider compacted gravel or tarred and shingled areas. They can look just as good, but keep them far enough from the house that gravel does not get tramped inside.

All you will need to maintain these areas will be weedkiller, and the occasional topping or resurfacing. Remember that all paved areas should have firm edges—crumbling paving means no saving of time or money at all. Timber which is rot-proofed will serve to make hard edges, though brick or stone is preferable. To break up an over-large gravelled or pebbled area, you can decorate it with other groups of

Top right. Two types of paving meet at right angles beside a smoothly-sloped lawn. A copper beech adds a note of rich colour to the prevailing expanses of greenery.
Below left. An elegant patio overlooking a simple oval lawn. Trees and roses are clustered close to the curving path to add interest at different levels.

pebbles, boulders, stepping stones, or just an occasional large piece of interestingly shaped rock as a focal point.

Another way of using gravel is in the formal garden, where geometric patterns of differently coloured aggregates can, for instance, be divided by courses of brick, stone setts, or timber.

Ha-Ha's

Fences or hedge lines can be ugly and unnecessary in a country garden, where they would interrupt the view to open countryside beyond. At the same time, animals have to be prevented from straying into your territory from neighbours' land. One single cow can do untold damage to a garden in the course of an afternoon stroll!

A ha-ha provides an effective answer to the problem. Basically, it is a ditch with a fence at the bottom. It has to be deep enough to conceal the fence from normal view, high enough to keep animals out, and wide enough to stop them jumping across. From the house (or other main viewing point) a lawn running to a ha-ha appears to run on, uninterrupted, into the grass-land beyond. It is an ideal way of integrating the landscape you might like to own with the garden you do.

A refinement of the ha-ha is a vertical wall in the ditch on the side nearer the house, high enough to keep animals—and other trespassers—out. The opposite side of the ditch can then be graded out gently, or sown down by you or your neighbour.

You will need to co-operate on this, of course. Unless you are prepared to lose part of your site, you will need permission to excavate and re-grade land outside your boundary. Legal wrangles can be expensive, and are never pleasant. But ha-ha's avoid the use of ugly fencing, and could well appeal to your neighbours, who would no longer need to maintain their part of the boundary.

Play areas

The main play area should generally be near the house, where the children can be watched, and near enough for an emergency rescue—not just a warning shout.

Children best appreciate paths without sharp corners so that they can easily be man-euvred by the inexpert tricyclist. Alternative routes to any main terrace, and ramps rather than steps, are ideal for the toddler to negotiate with his toy car or bike. (Ramps are also a boon for the elderly, who might find steps troublesome.) And children like winding paths—literally 'going round in circles'. They will play longer where there is uninterrupted access than where paths end in blind alleys.

Swings can be a problem. They are difficult to mow around, and the turf underneath inevitably wears out and looks scruffy. There is a type of double swing which has an ingenious 'split personality', converting to a swing hammock so it can be hooked aside for moving. About the turf problem you cannot do much; even bare ground is marginally less dangerous to fall on than concrete is.

When preparing the site you intend to be a play area, think twice before you throw out any old tree stumps or gnarled logs. They make excellent and much appreciated natural play-things for children, as well as integrating well with the garden surrounds.

The approach drive

First impressions make a much greater im-pact on visitors than either you or they may realize. On the one hand, you may not want the front of the house in full view from the road, to preserve privacy. But on the other, make sure that the visitor is left in no doubt where to park and where the front door is. Lighting can play an important part in ensuring that the drive entrances and the main doorway are obvious, and welcoming at all times.

If you plan an 'in' and 'out' drive, a turning circle or shunt, avoid the temptation to base

***Above.** A lily pool surrounded by trees and a rockery, providing a large garden with a corner that is cool and attractive.*

the minimum radius on the turning circle of your own car. Visitors may drive even larger cars and will not be as familiar with the place, so give them plenty of room to manoeuvre. You may also have to take into account the size of delivery vehicles, such as fuel trucks.

The entrance

You will probably want to get the car as close to the front door as possible in bad weather, but remember that gravel from a loose surface can be 'walked' into the house unless it is walked off on hard paving first.

Try to create enough space for a group of people to stand comfortably outside the porch without being in danger of stepping back on to plants in borders or containers.

Terraces and entertaining

If you entertain a lot, some of it is bound to take place outside in good weather. You will need a terrace of generous proportions to accommodate a fair number of people—and,

since they will probably be arriving in the evening, ensure that it is well lit. Soft, overly 'romantic' lighting can be dangerous. This applies particularly to steps and low retaining walls, which could be hazardous even in twilight, when the eye begins to play tricks.

Terrace seating

Unless you prefer the more flexible unfixed seating such as deckchairs, consider incorpora-ting fixed seating into the design of the terrace or patio. But if you do this, avoid the use of too much stone. A barbecue may give off a fair amount of heat, but a stone seat tends to remain cold, and can feel like marble!

Few people in Britain use timber on terraces. But, quite apart from its use in fixed-seat slatting, you may well consider, say, teak for step treads or even for decking. Timber is a lot warmer underfoot than stone, and is more pleasant to dance on. Timber is particularly good for 'flying' terraces, where the land slopes sharply, and where stone terracing would demand massive retaining walls and soil infill. It is particularly attractive and natural-looking, too, where the terrace or sundeck is surrounded by the tops of trees and their foliage.

Above. This crazy paved front garden is stepped to add interest. The frontage has ample space for parking—and is attractively laid out

Designs for front gardens

Your front garden is very much what you make it. You are often so busy altering, designing and decorating the inside of your house, that you completely fail to notice the state of the front garden. You don't need green fingers to have an attractive front garden. With a little effort and imagination you can create a garden to be proud of, and one that will give the visitor a pleasing introduction to the rest of your home.

Nowadays most front gardens are a bit on the small side. With a small front garden you will be faced with the problem of how to make the most of the available space, without making the layout too regular—and therefore boring. So many front gardens are laid out along very traditional lines—a small lawn in the centre surrounded by a border of wall flowers and rose trees, with perhaps a fairly barren flower bed in the middle of the lawn.

There are a number of ways in which you can make your garden interesting and attractive even if it is small or an awkward shape.

Paths

In many gardens the path to the front door consists of a rather shabby strip of cracked concrete which seriously detracts from the overall appearance of the garden. You might consider laying a path of crazy paving. This could be banked up with natural stone such as York sandstone on either side. Small rock plants growing in the cracks and contours of the stone will 'frame' the path, and make it an attractive feature of your garden.

If your garden has a wide frontage a straight path, either cutting through the middle of the lawn or at one side of it, will give a monotonous layout. The best solution is to lay a curving path across the garden, starting with the front gate at the opposite side to the front door. The path

Above. A sloping garden imaginatively created. Small rock plants and shrubs are used to avoid obstructing the view.

should be laid from the gate to the door in an 'S' bend. If your garden is very small, a gentle curve will still be better than a straight path.

Very often front gardens slope down quite steeply to the road. In this case you can terrace the garden on two or three levels in steps. The path could either be cut deep at the side of the terraced lawn, and the terrace banked with a brick or stone wall, or you could terrace it in line with the garden.

If you have not much time to spend looking after your garden, or you aren't very interested in gardening, consider paving the area. There are a number of natural stones which are suitable for paving—including York stone and certain kinds of slate. A cheaper alternative to natural stone is pre-cast concrete paving slabs. These are available in square and rectangular shapes, usually 18in. x 18in. (450mm x 450mm) and 24in. x 18in. (600mm x 450mm) in size, as well as in

round and hexagonal shapes. They also come in a number of colours besides grey. You should be careful when using coloured slabs, because they can often look bitty and garish. It is usually better to stick to grey slabs, with perhaps a regularly shaped pattern for an inset—using coloured slabs. Cutting slabs can be a tricky business but by careful use of a bolster to cut the line and a heavy mallet the desired shape can be achieved. If you wish you can order slabs ready cut from your local mason.

If your front garden is very large it can take on a monotonous appearance if paved all over. Paving can be broken up if you incorporate beds where flowers and shrubs can be planted. To do this omit a paving slab or slabs where you wish a bed to be. Some plants need more soil depth than others if they are to flourish, so be on the safe side and provide at least a 9in. (225mm) depth of well fertilized vegetable soil in each bed. An alternative to beds for a paved garden, is to build small rockeries here and there at random—on which many small plants will thrive. Provided the rockeries are not out of scale

to the rest of your garden they will act as out-crops from the flat paved garden and can be very restful and pleasing to the eye. Rockeries can be usefully incorporated into lawned gardens as well.

Pools, while being beautiful and very suitable for a back garden, are not usually a good idea in front gardens. Most houses have front gardens that face directly on to a street. Because of this a great deal of litter will be blown about and some of it will find its way into a pool. Also, pools are a great attraction for other people's children, which can be a bit of a nuisance, and sometimes dangerous.

If you intend to have a paved front garden, you will have to face the fact that space to plant flowers will be quite limited. A good solution is to grow flowers in large tubs. These tubs can be placed on level strips of concrete, or paving under windows. As well as tubs of flowers you could include window boxes and some hanging baskets.

Tubs, hanging baskets and window boxes also offer a very good solution to the small front

garden where room for planting will naturally be restricted.

It's not always a good idea to clutter up your garden with shrubs and plants, even if it is quite large. Creeping plants, growing over the front of your house, take up hardly any space and, at the same time improve the appearance if the front is otherwise quite plain.

Landscaping

A soft undulating garden can be a great deal more interesting and attractive than a totally level site. With the exception of traditional and formal layouts, landscaping a flat site will not be a success unless the levels of areas of the garden are altered to add a degree of realism to the layout. You will very soon find a completely flat site tedious to the eye. Carefully sited shapes and steps will provide a more stimulating and visually attractive outlook. If you landscape your garden so that it slopes away from the house on a gradual incline. it will mean that particular features can be seen to better advantage from a front window.

Above. This fairly traditional garden is given added interest by the well proportioned front wall and the attractively stepped path. *Inset.* Here the paved front garden is 'framed' by colourful flowers and shrubs.

If your garden slopes toward the house you will need to make special arrangements for drainage. Install a drain line running across the edge of the terrace. Water running off the garden will meet with water running off the terrace paving. Where a drain line ends in a soak hole place this as far as possible from the house. Land sloping toward the house shortens the view and can make large gardens seem small.

While ground sloping toward the house will make your garden seem smaller, the reverse is true if the land slopes away from the house—an impression of spaciousness will be achieved. The perspective will be deepened if this treatment is applied to a garden, and it will be especially effective if views over countryside or parkland exist. Plants and other features of this type of garden may not be visible from the house,

Opposite page. Here a beautiful weeping willow makes an impressive centre piece to this paved garden. It's often a good idea to make a display of this kind—especially in a small garden where little else can be planted.

but these features offer a pleasant surprise to visitor as he explores your garden.

Flat sites

With very flat front gardens, flower beds, tree and shrubs can be 'stepped' with low growin plants at the front and larger ones at the rea This will give the impression that the lan undulates slightly. However, even with lev sites a certain amount of landscaping may b desirable to give a more imaginative visual effec to your garden. If you wish to create an informa garden, concentrate on gentle rises and fall rather than steep and abrupt changes in land scape. With less dramatic contours, you ca successfully create a heathland or meadowlan atmosphere in your garden. Another advantag of gentle contours is that the grass can still b

own easily, and is therefore much easier to control.

The grading of the lawn landscape should be such that puddles don't collect in the dips. If you want a lawn to slope downwards to the centre is a good idea to have some plants or a rockery conceal a soakaway.

Small front gardens

In a very small front garden you should make all use of any vertical structure—garden walls, house walls, fences, screens and the like. The aim should be to provide a number of focal points at different levels.

Surprisingly enough, one good solution to designing a small front garden is to fill it with plants. You need to accept that you have no space to accommodate anything very much, so the accent should be on the purely decorative. Aim at having a lot of colourful flowers at eye level or just below. Window boxes at first floor level can also be very effective. If you concentrate purely on flower beds at ground level in a small garden, you will emphasize the restricted space and make the garden look tiny.

To have flower beds on different levels you will need to remove the topsoil then a foundation of hardcore must be laid to form the shape of a miniature landscape. The topsoil must then be replaced. As there will be a greater surface to cover you will need to provide more topsoil—either bought or taken from your back garden. Some form of paving between the beds will be not only decorative but essential. You should have a firm area to walk on when planting or weeding the beds.

Low level trellices, with creepers of various kinds intertwining, can be used attractively and originally in a small garden. They lead the eye on to discover the surprises in store behind each trellice.

As mentioned above, pools are not usually a good idea in a front garden. However, in a medium or large garden, which has been well landscaped, a small pool combined with a small waterfall coming from a rockery can look beautiful and achieve a sense of tranquility. For a waterfall, install an electrically operated pump.

If you have a small front garden and are not the least interested in gardening, you could consider paving it over, removing the front wall facing the road, and providing parking space for your car. As long as there is enough room to park the car so that no part of it obstructs the pavement this could be a solution for your problem garden. But remember that the roadside kerb will have to be removed, and the pavement bevelled. In Britain, this job must be carried out by the local authority.

Oddly shaped gardens with acute angles in the corners present another problem. Formal flowerbeds and hedges running parallel to the angle should be avoided. For the corners of a triangular garden, seats and rockeries offer the best solution to a tricky problem. In such a plot a lawn is often not a good idea. If you wish to have a lawn it will look much more in keeping with the site if it is made circular, with a paved area over the rest of the triangle.

With careful planning, your front garden can make your house more attractive even before you enter the front door.

Above. If your house is on a sloping site, you can easily create a rock garden. Left. Steps provide an ideal site for a rock garden.

Rock garden design

you are lucky enough to have a large rden, you can make it more attractive d interesting by dividing it up into ferent parts, incorporating various ids of plant, shrub and tree. You don't ed a lot of space to construct a rock garden, however, but if it is well planned and planted, it can be a most rewarding form of horticulture.

Rock gardens don't have to be enormous landscaped areas consisting of tons of large rocks, and in fact you can build one to a size to suit the proportions of your particular garden, whether large or small. In the past, the stones were given more importance than the plants, which meant that many good plant specimens died, but there are many attractive plants which thrive in a rockery, and are not difficult to cultivate; most of them are alpine varieties.

Alpine plants

Although it is not essential to build a rock garden in order to grow alpine plants, it is obviously a pleasant feature to add to any garden with a suitable site, and alpines always look better growing in their natural surroundings.

29

BILL MCLAUGHLIN

With a few exceptions, alpine plants are not difficult to grow at all, if they are given a chance by being positioned where they are likely to thrive. They will put up with a variety of conditions, but there are three basic rules to observe which, if ignored, can result in their death.

Alpine plants will not survive in sour and badly drained soil; they will not grow where water drips continually from the branches of overhanging trees; and they will not endure draughts or cutting winds.

Siting a rock garden

Most gardens should have a suitable situation for a rock garden, as there are few hard and fast rules about siting. Ideally you should choose a gentle slope falling to the south or south west, or as near as possible. Avoid a due east aspect, as the east wind harms most plants.

Naturally it is unwise to choose a site which is exposed to strong prevailing cold winds, or flooding after heavy rain, but an exposed site can be sheltered a certain amount by shrubs and small trees planted near enough to act as a windbreak, but not so close as to overshadow it.

As with most gardens, it is important that the soil is well drained, which is generally the case on a slope anyway. If the ground you have chosen is flat, you may have to insert land drains or some other aid to drainage.

As a rock garden is chiefly a decorative feature, you will probably want it to be as near the house as possible, or at least visible from the house. However, if it is going to be a large landscaped area, it may be better to place it

further away from the more formal part of the garden which usually surrounds a house.

Your choice of plants will also have an important bearing on the siting of a rock garden. Plants which enjoy a cool situation will obviously not live happily in the same conditions as those which thrive under a Mediterranean sun. If you cannot find a site which offers a wide variety of aspects, you will be more limited in your choice of plants.

A popular choice of site for a rock garden is a steep bank or grassy slope which is difficult to cut. Here you have a naturally sloping site which should be well drained and open in aspect. This kind of situation often lends itself to the addition of water in the form of a waterfall or pool, which will improve the appearance of a rock garden.

Finally, you should bear in mind that large amounts of rock, and perhaps soil, will have to be transported to the site, and that there should be an easy means of access to it. A lawn can be carved up badly by trucks with heavy loads being driven across it, so it is worth seeing if you can't position your rock garden near a path.

Suitable rocks

Wherever possible it is preferable to use local stone for a rock garden, for both aesthetic and economic reasons. If your house, or a garden wall, is built in local stone, a rock garden in the same material will blend in better with its surroundings. Equally important is the cost of transporting stone from one part of the country to another.

Above left. Several individual rock garden set in a lawn make a pleasant change on a flat site from conventional flower beds. An attractive idea is to form narrow grass paths which run between the rock gardens, which help to create a more landscaped appearance. *Above.* Here a larger and mor

It is wise to avoid using limestone near lar towns and cities, as the effect of polluted produces a hard, marble-like whiteness whi stands out harshly. If local stone does not ex in your part of the country, you will have choose from what is available from a comme cial source. Always choose natural stor whatever the cost, and don't be tempted by t apparent economy of substitutes such broken concrete, smashed masonry or brick which will eventually have to be replaced wi natural stone.

Soil

If you are constructing a landscaped ro garden on a flat site, you will naturally need f more soil than if you are converting an existi slope. However, if the natural soil is not goc you may have to remove a certain amount ar replace it with something more suitable. As far quantities are concerned, you can usually wo on the basis that for each ton of stone you us you will need a cubic yard of compost.

A simple compost which will suit most alpi plants consists of loam, humus and grit. Loa is the bulk constituent, and if stacked, fibro loam is not available, any good top-spit so

...borate rockery forms the focal point of ...s sloping garden, with some rough steps ...corporated into it. **Above right.** If your ...use is set high above the road, a rockery ...kes an original front garden. Here shallow ...ks have been used for informal steps, ...ergrown with fast-spreading rock plants.

...ich is reasonably friable will do. It is worth ...ing the trouble to get a good quality loam, ...d not accept a cheap substitute.

...Humus can take the form of leaf mould, well-...ted garden compost, or a fine-grade granu-...ed moss peat. Avoid sedge peat if possible, as ...s more acid and seldom breaks down into the ...er granules of moss peat. Grit can consist of ...arp sand or fine stone chippings. Don't use ...low builder's sand, which is a false economy. ...e grit must be a sharp, non-binding material, ...ce its function is to provide an 'open', ...ickly draining compost.

...You can make a standard compost using the ...ove ingredients by mixing 4 parts of loam with ...arts of humus and 1½ parts of grit, all parts by ...lk. For those areas of a rock garden where you ...nt to grow more choice plants, the grit can be ...reased to 2 or even 2½ parts.

...Before mixing the materials, dust the whole ...generously with bone meal, using approx-...ately 7lbs to each cubic yard of compost. ...x the ingredients thoroughly by turning them ...veral times, and then cover the soil until it is ...eded, to avoid either saturation or aridity ...used by the elements.

...You should be able to amend this basic compost to suit the needs of all the plants you choose for your rock garden. It is possible to buy ready-made soil mixtures, but these often work out too expensive for a rock garden, since you will probably have to buy all the plants at the same time. If you cannot get suitable materials, a good John Innes potting mixture formula can be used, provided it comes from a reliable source.

Preparing the site

It is vital that a site for a rock garden is prepared correctly in the first place, as mistakes are difficult to remedy later on without under-taking major reconstruction work. With all the materials close at hand, you should set about preparing the site.

If the drainage is not satisfactory, you must see to it that no surplus water will linger where it is not wanted, among the roots of alpine plants. If the soil is very heavy, it should be replaced with coarse drainage of some kind. If the soil is basically good, then all you need to do is to dig it over and clean it thoroughly, remov-ing all perennial weeds and their roots.

If you are planning to incorporate some form of water feature, you must naturally complete all the construction of any pipes and concrete pools before building the rockery. If you are using glassfibre pools or plastic sheeting, these can be incorporated during the construction.

Designing the layout

Before you start any actual construction work, you should draw up a rough plan of the general outline of your rock garden. Decide where the principal features are to be, where any paths are to go, and mark these out with stakes. You will not be able to plan exactly where each stone goes, and you will have to design as you go along, but it is important to try to arrange them so that they seem to have grown together naturally.

It helps a great deal if you can see a few good rock gardens first and study the arrangement of stones carefully to get a few tips. The first stone is the most difficult to place, but if you proceed slowly, you should be able to construct a natural-looking arrangement. Wherever possible you should try to make the rock garden blend in well with its surroundings, but in any event if it is well constructed it should not stand out badly if this is not feasible.

It is easier to build a rock garden on a slope, which lends itself to the appearance you are trying to achieve. A flat site needs more imagination if you are to create an illusion of peaks and valleys. It is important that the line of slope of all the rocks should be in the same direction, also that they are placed in close association to each other.

If you are incorporating paths into the layout of your rock garden, you may have to connect them to each other or with the surrounding ground by steps. If possible these steps should by composed of the same stone that you are using for the rock garden. Some stones can be split easily to the appropriate thickness for steps, others will have to be buried to a conveni-ent depth.

While building a rock garden, it is important to remember that many of the plants you are going to grow there thrive best in the narrow crevices between the rocks. As it is difficult to insert them after the rock garden is finished, you may find it preferable to plant some during construction. The main planting should be left until some time after completion, so as to allow enough time for the compost to settle firmly in place, but you can fit in crevice-loving plants as you create an appropriate position.

Rock garden plants

There is a very wide variety of plants which can be grown in a rock garden, and many that are not strictly 'alpine' nevertheless enjoy the conditions and look appropriate in such surroundings. If you have not cultivated rock plants before, it is perhaps wise to start with the more easily grown ones.

Whereas plants like *arabis, alyssum* and *aubrietia* provide splendid colour and growth in the spring, you should try to choose plants which give interest all the year round. Here is a list of some sun-loving plants which are quite easy to grow in a rock garden.

The various species of *acaena* are excellent carpeting plants, but they should not be placed close to small plants, which they would swamp with their somewhat exuberant growth. They are invaluable for planting in the chinks between flat stones in a path, or as ground cover for bulbs in open areas.

Several of the rock garden *achilleas* are useful for providing carpets of attractive foliage,

Above. *Where a rock garden covers a larger area, and is on a steeper slope, it is safer to construct a wider, more formal flight of steps. It is also wise to keep the rock plants from growing over the steps.*

covered in early summer with showy flowers.

An attractive small shrub for a rock garden is *aethionema* ('Warley Rose'), whose woody branches are covered from early summer onwards with hundreds of small, deep pink flowers.

The exception to the rule about *alyssum* is *alyssum spinosum*, whose spiky bushes are smothered for weeks in mid-summer with either white or very soft pink flowers.

There are superior forms of the common thrift, *armeria maritima*, which are suitable for a rock garden. 'Vindictive', 'Bloodstone' and 'Merlin' are three excellent kinds with flowers ranging from deep pink to red, and *armeria maritima alba* is a useful albino.

There are many different rock garden *campanulas* from which you can choose, most of which are colourful and fast growing.

Dianthus of all kinds follow the early spring display of other plants, and you can plant them generously.

Another prostrate shrub suitable for a rock garden is *dryas octopetala*, which drapes its woody stems over warm rocks, and has attractive white flowers.

Gentians are not as hard to grow as is commonly believed, in particular *gentian septemfida* and *gentian acaulis*.

Some varieties of *geranium*, such as *gerani subcaulescens, geranium renardii* and *gerani dalmaticum*, provide compact ground cover rock garden, combined with colourful flowers

The sun roses, or *helianthemums*, provide wide choice, which enjoy a very hot, dry site tion. These are shrubby plants which flower summer, and are available in a wide range colours.

The yellow *hypericum rhodopeum* is a use plant for permanent effect in a rock garden.

Alpine *phloxes* are indispensable, and th are many varieties which form low, tuf cushions, in all sorts of colours.

From the *saxifrage* genus you can choo plants for sun and shade, also for early and l flowering. These also come in a wide variety colours.

Foliage plants are valuable in a rock gard and you should be able to find many suita varieties at your local garden centre. One su able plant is *artemisia lanata*, which provides attractive ground cover of silver leaves.

Don't be tempted to buy plants which gr very quickly because you want to cover the b expanse of rocks and soil as soon as possib Some fast-growing plants develop such a f roothold that most of the rock garden needs be dismantled in order to remove them.

Remember that building and planting a r garden is a major undertaking which should dealt with seriously. If you take the trouble plan your site, rock arrangement and planti you will create an attractive garden feat which will give you years of pleasure.

Kitchen gardens

here are few experiences more satisfy-
ing than picking and eating fruit and
vegetables you have grown yourself.
Even the smallest garden can make room
for a few herbs, lettuces, radishes and
beetroots, which can be tucked in
among the ornamental plants. The globe
artichoke, a magnificent plant, is edible
as well as being very beautiful when in
flower, and later on it can be dried for
winter flower arrangements.

In the average sized garden it is usually
possible to arrange for a small area to be devoted
to fruit and vegetables, and this can easily be
separated from the main garden. A suitable
screen could consist of espalier apple or pear
trees, a trellis with climbing roses growing along
it, or a productive one of loganberries or
cultivated blackberries such as Oregon Thorn-
less, which can also be trained along the
boundary fences.

A sunny little bed near the back door is an
ideal place for a few herbs such as parsley,
chives, thyme, sage and (planted in a buried
receptacle to contain the roots) mint.

If space is limited it pays to be very dis-
criminating as to what you grow. Your best plan
is to choose such vegetables as are expensive,
rare or difficult to buy really fresh. For example,
baby French beans are rarely to be seen in any
but the most exclusive greengrocers and are
expensive; and lettuce and purple sprouting
broccoli often look very tired in the shops.

Soft fruit is very expensive and extremely
perishable, but it is surprising how many
raspberries can be grown in quite a small place.
Climbing French beans, variety Blue Lake, come
in later than the dwarf varieties and have the
advantage that, if you cannot pick regularly, they
do not go stringy as do scarlet runners. Just
topped and tailed, tossed in butter and a little
pepper, they are delicious eaten whole; moreover they deep freeze extremely well. There may
well come a time when gooseberries will be
unobtainable because of the difficulty of getting
pickers.

Planning the vegetable garden

If you decide to make a vegetable garden, an
open sunny situation is essential. Tall trees will
rob plants of food, and the shade from tall
buildings will cause thin lanky growth. Arrange
for the rows to run north and south to allow the
maximum amount of sun to shine on the plants
and to prevent the taller plants, i.e. peas and
beans, from casting shadows on their neighbours.
Before beginning to dig, sit down and plan
your layout on squared paper. Allowance must

be made for a compost heap, on which you will
put your lawn mowings, kitchen waste, including
vegetable peelings, tea leaves, dust from the
vacuum cleaner and anything else that will rot
down to make good organic food for your soil.

Below. *A popular site for a kitchen garden
is at the end of the main plot, screened from
the rest of the garden by a hedge. Herbs are
growing in the paved area near the house.*

If you can obtain animal manure easily and
cheaply, include a place for a heap of this
valuable material.

A tool shed will be needed, and a frame for
raising seeds or hardening off plants in. A
greenhouse, if you have one, is extremely useful,
and it is helpful to have a small area in shade for
a nursery bed. Remember that the tool shed and
greenhouse, and possibly the frames, are visited
in winter and wet weather, so construct a good
path to enable you to go dryshod.

Paths should be kept to a minimum because
they are wasteful of space, but good permanent
paths, wide enough for access with a wheel-
barrow to the compost or manure heaps, tool
shed, frame or greenhouse are essential. Good
advance planning of this kind cuts down work
later on.

You may wish to have a go at growing early
vegetables, in which case you will need some
cloches, which need storage space. Although
continuous cloches are less durable than the
individual ones, they take up less storage space
and are perfectly adequate. While the compost
and manure heaps are almost better in shade,
the frames and greenhouse must have a sunny
open position.

Do not forget such permanent crops as
rhubarb and asparagus if you have the space and
are likely to stay long enough in your house to
justify the outlay and work. Asparagus takes a
long time to come into bearing from seed, which
is the cheapest method of raising plants. Two-
year-old plants, the best, should not be cut the
first year, and are not cheap to buy. The bed
must be raised above the level of the ground, as
the plants are planted deeply and need good
drainage. An established asparagus bed is a very
pleasant thing to own and the fern is popular
with flower arrangers.

Digging the plot

If you want to grow good fruit and vegetables,
thorough preparation of the soil is essential. Do
not leave this until you see the first cabbage
plants and packets of seeds in the shops, but
spread the work over the autumn and fine days
in winter. This gives the frost and snow time to
work on your behalf by breaking down the
roughly dug soil, so that when in March and
April you will be wanting to rake the soil into a
fine tilth for seed sowing, you can enjoy doing
this without having to rush to dig it in unsuitable
weather.

Soil which has already been cultivated will
probably need little more than digging over, one
spit deep (i.e. 10in., the depth of a spade). In
autumn lime the part you intend to use for
brassicas, i.e. the cabbage family, then use a

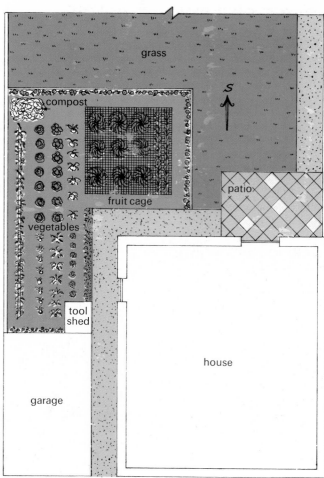

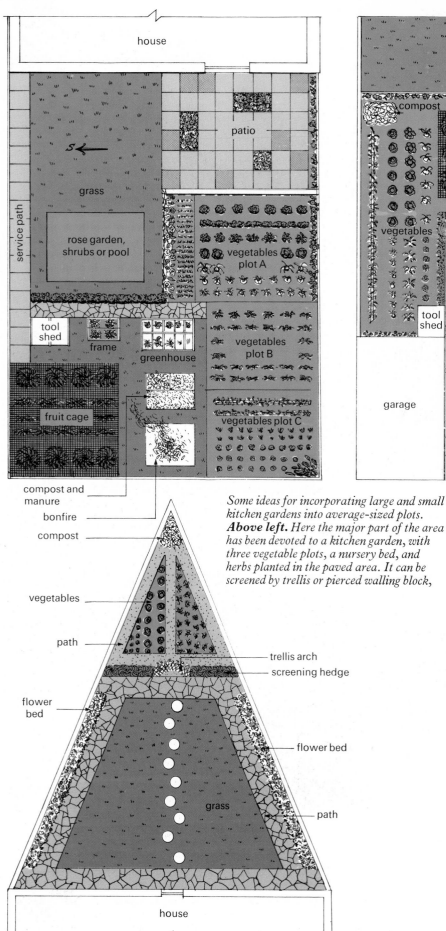

Some ideas for incorporating large and small kitchen gardens into average-sized plots.
Above left. Here the major part of the area has been devoted to a kitchen garden, with three vegetable plots, a nursery bed, and herbs planted in the paved area. It can be screened by trellis or pierced walling block, and the boundary fences are covered with climbing plants and espalier trees.
Above right. Here the vegetable garden occupies a small area at the side of a semi-detached house. It can be screened by cordon espalier or apple trees, climbing roses or a flowering hedge, and the garage wall is covered with loganberries or blackberries.
Left. The proportions of an awkward, angular plot can be improved by fitting a vegetable garden into one corner. Paths run round the edges, which are frequently in shadow. A screening hedge of bushes or cordon fruit trees hides it from the rest of the garden.

general fertilizer just before planting. Incorpora[te] manure in the pea and bean trenches, but do n[ot] add any manure to ground that will be used [for] root crops.

If the soil is covered with grass and wee[ds] and has not been cultivated for some time, [it] should be double dug, burying the grass a[nd] weeds in the lower spit.

If you have bought a new house, the lik[e]lihood is that there will be rubble and bric[k] lying about, and in digging the foundations, [the] infertile sub-soil may have been brought to t[he] surface. This will have buried the good da[rk] top-soil, which will have to be uncovered a[nd] brought to the surface. Trenching is the meth[od] used for getting the various soil layers into th[e] proper place.

Whichever method you use, incorporate [as] much organic matter as possible, i.e. gra[ss] mowings, leaves or compost, to improve t[he] texture and drainage of the soil.

JOHN DAWES

Crop rotation

Although not essential, it is wise to practise a three year crop rotation plan. Certain plants attract pests and diseases, and if the ground is continually used for the same crop a serious infestation can build up, notably club root disease in the cabbage family.

Crops also have different feeding requirements, and even help each other, as in the case of peas and beans, which leave valuable nitrate

Above. Runner beans make a good screen for one side of a kitchen garden, being both decorative and productive. Rows of beetroots and parsnips are growing in front of it here.

in the soil. This is needed by the cabbage family, which should succeed the peas and beans the following year. The chart below will act as a guide to cropping and manuring.

If it is not possible to carry out crop rotation,

the soil must be given plenty of manure if you want to grow the greedy feeders, i.e. peas and beans, and generous liming of the ground in all but alkaline soils will be necessary if brassicas are grown to a great extent. Prevention against club root disease should also be taken, such as the use of calomel dust when planting out.

Where space is limited, inter-cropping can be practised, and fast maturing plants such as lettuce, radish, mustard and cress can be sown

between rows of peas, beans, cabbages etc, while they are still small. The catch crop, as it is called, is cleared away before the main crop needs the full space available. Adequate manure or fertilizer as appropriate must be given where there is intensive cropping, otherwise the plants will be of poor quality.

The herb garden

Most herbs need good drainage and a sunny situation. They look pretty and can be grown in many ways. The various varieties of thyme are suitable for inserting in crevices in paving or in dry stone walls; chives are attractive in groups in the flower border; parsley has pretty foliage; and sage has good-looking grey leaves.

Those herbs most likely to be used for cooking should be handy for the kitchen. A charming herb garden can be made, using these and many others such as rosemary, rue, fennel, marjoram, tarragon and lavender, and a fragrant bed or border with a bird bath in the middle can be a most attractive feature in any garden.

The fruit garden

If you have space, a separate area devoted to fruit is very profitable. Protection from birds is essential and, as in the case of the kitchen garden, rows should run north and south for maximum sunlight.

A fruit cage is the most satisfactory form of protection from birds, but also the most expensive. Squirrels will eat through plastic netting, so if these pests are present in your garden, ¾in. mesh wire netting will keep out squirrels and deter most birds. Plastic netting of

Above. This vegetable garden has been laid out neatly in labelled rows, set at right angles to a central path for easy access. The screen hedge provides shelter from winds.

the same mesh can be put over the top just before the fruit ripens, but it should be removed for winter, otherwise snow will damage it. A 6ft high cage is best, so that you do not have to bend when working in it.

Portable metal frames in various sizes are on the market, or you can make one out of wooden posts at least 7ft 6in. tall, driven 18in. into the ground and spaced 6ft apart throughout the cage. Black, red and white currants, raspberries, gooseberries and strawberries are easily grown. They don't involve much work, apart

from pruning and manuring and, in the case raspberries, being supported with wire to whi the canes are tied.

Apple and pear trees on dwarfing stoc which prevent them from growing too tall especially suitable for small gardens, and ma spraying, pruning and fruit picking much easi Some varieties of apple and pear are self-ster which means that they need another varie which flowers at the same time to act as pollinator to fertilize them. Your nurserym should be able to advise you as to whi varieties to grow together, and on those whi are likely to do well in your neighbourhood.

This chapter should encourage you to e periment a bit and enjoy a useful and healt hobby suitable for all the family.

1st year plan

Plot	Cropping	Manuring
A	Broccoli, brussels sprouts, cabbages, cauliflower, kale, turnips etc.	Lime in autumn, unless soil is alkaline. Dig in manure or compost during winter.
B	Peas, beans, onions, shallots, leeks, celery.	Manure.
C	Early potatoes, carrots, beet, parsnips, swedes, spinach.	Light dressing of general fertilizer (e.g. Growmore) before sowing.

2nd year plan

Crops in Plot A will go into Plot B, those in Plot B into Plot C, and those in Plot C into Plot A. The manuring will be done for the crops as appropriate.

3rd year plan

Plot B into Plot C, Plot C into Plot A, and Plot A into Plot B.

4th year plan

Start from the beginning again with the manuring plan as appropriate to the crop.

LESLIE JOHNS

Above. This formal pool is incorporated with a small paved sitting-out area and low wall, making it a major feature of the garden which is visible from the house.

Water gardens

any people think that, just because eir garden is not very large, a water ature is out of the question. There are any types of water gardens, comprising ols, streams, waterfalls and fountains, hich can be incorporated into any rden to improve its appearance.

An attractive pool, once filled with plants and fish, can soon become a feature of your garden, no matter how small it is. The important point to remember is to design a pool whose shape and size fit in well with your particular garden.

For instance, if your garden has rounded

lines, with winding paths running here and there, a curved or circular pool will be more suitable than a harsh angular one. Conversely, a square pool often looks best in a rectangular garden.

The general appearance of a very flat garden can be greatly improved by constructing a raised pool, and then landscaping its surround. A good scheme here is to incorporate the pool into a rockery, thus creating a completely integrated area. There are more ideas for rock gardens which you can develop for yourself with a little imagination. It is possible for example to include a raised pool in the design.

If your garden is already landscaped in an

You can even buy glassfibre bases which fo rock pools, streams and waterfalls, which hav rugged finish to them.

The strongest garden pool is the tradition one made of concrete, but it involves mc expense and hard work, and needs clo attention to detail.

Once the hole has been excavated, y should insert a thick layer of hardcore and be it down well to form a firm base for t concrete. The concrete should be reinforc with some steel mesh, and then covered with rendering coat.

As concrete contains free lime, a preparati

Left. This water feature has been given an unusual treatment using natural timber for the surround and bridge, and sections of tree trunk for stepping stones.

COLIN WATMOUGH

interesting manner, you can take advantage of the various different levels by forming a stream which runs down preformed channels set between stones. It is quite simple to incorporate a waterfall or two in this type of water garden, all leading down to a decorative pool.

If you feel your garden would benefit from the addition of an ornament, you could fix a statue in the pool, or even more than one. Some of these can be connected to the water supply, particularly figures of animals such as lions and dolphins, allowing the water to pour from their mouths.

A popular, and most effective, feature of a water garden is a fountain set in a pool. There are many available which produce a wide variety of different jets and sprays. Some fountain jets can be mounted on to an artificial stone figure, which adds an even more dramatic touch to your water garden.

Garden pools

Many people think constructing a pool and installing a water feature involves a huge amount of expense, but this need not be the case.

There are three main types of pool available, and their cost reflects their relative strength and durability. But there are other considerations to bear in mind when planning a water garden, which will also affect your choice.

Any home handyman should be able to excavate a suitable hole to act as the basis for a pool, and it is a simple job to fit either plastic sheeting or a glassfibre pool, whereas a concrete pool involves more time and effort.

Flexible plastic sheeting allows for great freedom of design, and is particularly suitable where an informal shape is wanted. There are various materials available which are reasonably tough and can even be patched if punctured. Polythene pool liners are very fragile and should only be used for a temporary pool.

The flat sheets of plastic need no fixing, but are held in position by water pressure. The plastic moulds itself to the shape of the excavation, and the edges are covered with stones to give a natural finished appearance.

Prefabricated glassfibre pools are more expensive than flexible pools, but are more durable and very easy to install. They are particularly good where you find difficulty in digging a well-shaped hole because of either very soft or hard, stony ground.

Glassfibre pools are available in a wide range of designs to suit gardens of all shapes and sizes. They are usually between 1ft and 2ft deep, and most have a shallower 'shelf' round the perimeter which takes marginal aquatic plants.

Some of these have a tough surround moulded to simulate crazy paving or rockery stones, which help them blend in better with their surroundings. These cost more than the plain types, but avoid the need to buy additional edging materials, which are expensive.

Right. A courtyard garden is an attractive feature in a modern house as here, where a formal pool is surrounded by pebbles. The harsh outline is softened by plants.

...ust be used to neutralize it before plants and ...sh are placed in the pool. If cracks occur in the ...urface of a concrete pool, it is sometimes ...ossible to repair them. If they persist, however, ...e best plan is to line the whole pool with ...astic sheeting, which will stretch to the shape ...f any pool and can be easily fitted with a little ...are and patience.

If you don't feel inclined to go to the ...xpense of buying a proper garden pool, you ...an create your own using an old glazed ...reclay kitchen sink. You can give it a mossy ...ppearance by the application of a mixture ...alled Hypatufa, the ingredients of which

Right. Most of this small town garden has ...een devoted to a pond with water lilies ...rowing in it. Goldfish, marginal plants and ...tiny fountain all add further interest.

IRIS HARDWICK

DOUGLAS SIMMONDS

can be found at your local stockist. Plants eventually cling to a sink finished with this substance, and it will soon blend in well with its surroundings.

Pool plants

Water lilies (*Nymphaea*) are the best known plants used in garden pools, and there are many varieties suitable for all sizes of pool. They grow with their roots in mud at the bottom of ponds, with their foliage and flowers on the surface.

Most are perfectly hardy, but those from tropical regions need at least frost protection in winter indoors. The following types will grow quite easily in most garden pools.

Nymphaea alba (common water lily), *Nymphaea candida*, *Nymphaea fennica* and *Nymphaea nitida* all have flowers which bloom in summer.

Nymphaea odorata has white flowers tinged with red, which open in the morning and close after midday; and *Nymphaea pygmaea alba* has white flowers with golden stamens. *Nymphaea helvola*, the smallest water lily, has primrose yellow flowers; *Nymphaea tuberosa* has white flowers, and the *rosea* variety has pale rose flowers.

Submerged and floating aquatic plants are vital for the well-being of a pool to correct the balance and obtain clear water. Oxygenating aquatics replace lost oxygen to the water and provide cover and a breeding ground for the fish.

The majority of hardy marginal plants like to have their roots covered with 2 or 3in. of water, although some will grow in more and others are

perfectly happy in permanently wet soil. You should be able to find suitable species in the following genera: *Acorus, Butomus, Caltha* (*Caltha palustris plena*, the double marsh marigold, is excellent for planting at the water's edge), *Cotula, Cyperus, Eriophorum, Iris, Juncus, Menyanthes, Mimulus* (*Mimulus luteus*, the monkey musk, roots below the water and is a perennial which makes a good display in summer), *Orontium, Pontederia, Sagittaria, Scirpus* and *Typha*.

Some plants have to be put in containers, as many glassfibre pools do not retain the soil on the shelves. Many pool plants, particularly water lilies, need to be chosen and planted with great care, so it is wise to consult your nurseryman before making any hasty decisions.

A good edging plant is *Myriophyllum proserpinacoides*, which is a very rampant grower. It soon disguises the edge of the pool and overhangs the water.

Fish

Fish not only provide an attractive feature in a garden pool, but also help maintain the balance of life. In particular they control mosquito larvae. They consume numerous pests of water plants, such as aphids, moths, caddis flies and lily beetles, and their excreta helps fertilize aquatic plants. Their respiratory processes provide carbon dioxide used by oxygenating plants during photosynthesis.

Don't overcrowd a pool with too many fish, or they will die. A safe maximum quantity can be worked out on the basis of one inch of fish to every gallon of water.

The most popular, and most suitable, species for ornamental ponds is the common goldfish. They are very hardy and come in a wide range of colours from silver to rich gold and almost black, some in a combination of all these colours. They lay their eggs in early summer, and the fry appear very dark on hatching, but assume their permanent colours after two or three years.

The shubunkin is a scaleless goldfish, and has the attraction of being available in red, white, blue, pink or mauve, or a combination of any or all of these colours.

The golden orfe is particularly hardy, and suitable for almost any pond or lake. It ranges from 2in. to 2ft in length and soon becomes tame enough to feed from the hand. It has a silver underside and golden-salmon coloured back, and swims near the surface in shoals at great speed.

The golden rudd is very similar to orfe, both in shape and habit, but is silver all over with dark brown and sometimes bright red fins.

Above. A fountain adds a dramatic touch to any water feature. Here the geometric formality of a hexagonal pool is offset by the unusual crystal sculpture in the centre. The trees behind provide a soft background.

Fish bring life and movement to a water garden, but you should also add certain forms of molluscs, which perform a useful purpose. They act as scavengers and consume unwanted debris such as algae, fish excreta, food remains, dead creatures etc.

The best of these is the ramshorn snail (*Planorbis corneus*), which has a shell like a ram's horn. There are several other varieties available, but the freshwater whelk (*Limnaea stignaliis*) consumes many floating and sub-merged oxygenating plants and should be removed from the pool wherever possible.

Lighting

Whereas the sun glints attractively on water

by day, at night your water feature dies unl you enhance it with the use of artificial lighti You can greatly improve the look of a wa garden by illuminating it after dark.

If you have a fountain in your pool, it c come alive at night with the aid of colou floodlights. These should be directed on to pool from behind or from the sides, and c quite easily be concealed in the undergrov surrounding the pool.

Some lights will float on the surface of a po and others can be submerged, and directed into a fountain or cascade. It is essential take expert advice when using electricity this way, as it can be dangerous.

Use some of the ideas given here to form yo own water garden, but be careful to keep it proportion to the amount of land you have a its surrounding landscape. If your water feat is near the house, you can sit indoors and en the spectacle that you have created both by and by night.

PAUL KEMBLE

Above. *A really grand roof garden, so well planned that it looks like a ground-level garden—until you see the impressive panorama surrounding the building.*

The elevated garden

A roof garden is a feature that can lend individuality and character to your home. For one thing, the location of the garden, whether on a window ledge, balcony, flat roof, or the wide flat edge round an apex roof, can impart a unique quality to it. For another, different soils can be used, providing a growing medium for a wider range of plants than would be possible in the average garden. And if plants are grown in individual containers these can be moved if required, altering the whole layout of the garden.

A roof garden is an asset to your home—even if you already have a ground-level garden. If you possess a gardenless town house, you could install a realistic garden on the roof; and if you already have a garden you could create something intentionally artificial and visually different.

Structural considerations

Regardless if any alterations are intended, before planning a roof garden you should get expert advice on whether the roof structure is strong enough to take the extra weight involved. Large quantities of moist soil will place a severe strain on the area required to support it.

Some structural alterations are beyond the scope of the home handyman. For instance, the removal of an apex roof to provide a flat expanse—as is often done for buildings in the middle of town—will require steel girders and joists slung to carry the weight of the new structure.

The actual roof surface must be sufficiently thick and waterproof to withstand both constant contact with moisture and the considerable pressures exerted by the hard edges of heavy containers.

There must also be a means of efficient drainage, and you should investigate local bye-laws and landlord's agreements, if necessary, to find out if there is a ban on roof gardening.

The considerable time and expense involved in obtaining expert advice on the physical and legal aspects are well worth while. If you do not do this, you could be involved in a lawsuit, or worse, part of the building might collapse.

Safety

Safety is a prime consideration in roof garden design, especially if children are present. The roof you have in mind may have a surrounding parapet or wall that is sufficiently high to deter children from climbing over, but such walls are rare. Railings of some sort must usually be provided. If you have a parapet wall, however low, it may be possible to bolt posts to it. This will enable you to build a wooden fence inside the wall and simulate a ground level garden.

Practical considerations

The problems of roof gardening are entirely different from those encountered at ground level. Basically the main difference is in the depth of soil. At ground level plants grow in soil that has greater depth, even though the productive surface may only be a few inches deep. Even in the driest weather there exists, under ground level plants, a reservoir of moisture from which roots can absorb water.

On the roof, soil is necessarily so shallow that moisture drains away quickly and can be replaced only by constant watering as there is no underground supply from which to draw. This also means that essential plant foods and minerals will be quickly leached by watering, and nutrients lost must be replaced with greater frequency than is necessary at ground level. Shallow soil also prohibits the growth of thick, strong anchoring roots, so large trees and shrubs cannot normally be grown to maturity. While young, however, some can be used to provide cover for low growing vegetation.

Effects of weather

Roof gardens are likely to be affected by changes in weather. The sun is always hotter on the roof, and the rain more concentrated. Wind presents a special problem. The increased force at roof level will tear at the taller plants such as shrubs, and as they are not so deeply rooted as ground level plants they can actually be dislodged when the wind is high. For this reason, a good fence, in addition to being visually attractive, can act as a buffer.

On the other hand, a roof garden is usually warmer in winter, because of the slight heat rising from the building.

Visual aspects

Roof gardening is an artificial form of gardening and, as such, you can get away with certain design features that would look out of place at ground level. On the other hand, a roof garden with a tall wooden fence surrounding it, bordered by medium height shrubs and tall flowers, and laid with lawn, could simulate a ground level garden exactly.

But although you may be able to afford some artificial features, do not fall into the trap of going too far in the opposite direction and trying to make things look too naturalistic. An artificial mound or 'hill', for example, is rarely successful and only imposes an even greater strain on the roof structure.

By using decorative containers you can utilize an important characteristic of all roof gardens—that is, the freedom to change the design or balance of the garden at any time by re-arranging the containers. These containers can be purchased in a variety of materials such as wood, stone, metal or plastic. Wooden tubs or barrels are particularly suitable, but they should be treated with a proprietary preservative. Holes should be bored in the bottoms for easy drainage and castors fixed to facilitate easy movement.

Containers look neatest if they are all made of the same material. But if different types of container are used a lot of character can be added if you have a sense of design—if you haven't, mixed containers can look a mess.

If the containers are not attractive in their own right, it is best to arrange them around the edges of the roof and to build a low wall or fence on the inside. This could be either a fence of vertical tongued-and-grooved boarding, or a wall of ornamental brickwork.

In some cases it is possible to place soil

Right. A composite picture showing three different types of fencing or walling. The base is composed of asbestos tiles over three layers of roofing felt. The canopy, if required, could easily be converted into a pergola for climbing plants such as roses, clematis, or honeysuckle. **a.** Method for 'flashing' the roof dpc into the parapet brickwork. At least three layers of felt are required. **b.** A 'set' of garden pools constructed from marine plywood and lined with fibreglass. The water is pumped from the bottom pool and up through the fountain head, creating a series of waterfalls. **c.** One method of fixing rail bottoms. The grey layer is sealing mastic. **d.** Wood battens glued to deck-chair webbing with contact adhesive make a flexible fence. Containers are placed over battens fixed to the support struts to prevent the wind blowing the fence over. **e.** The operation of the direct feed automatic watering system.

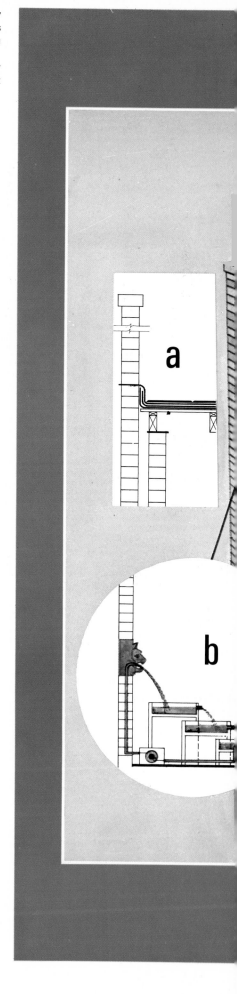

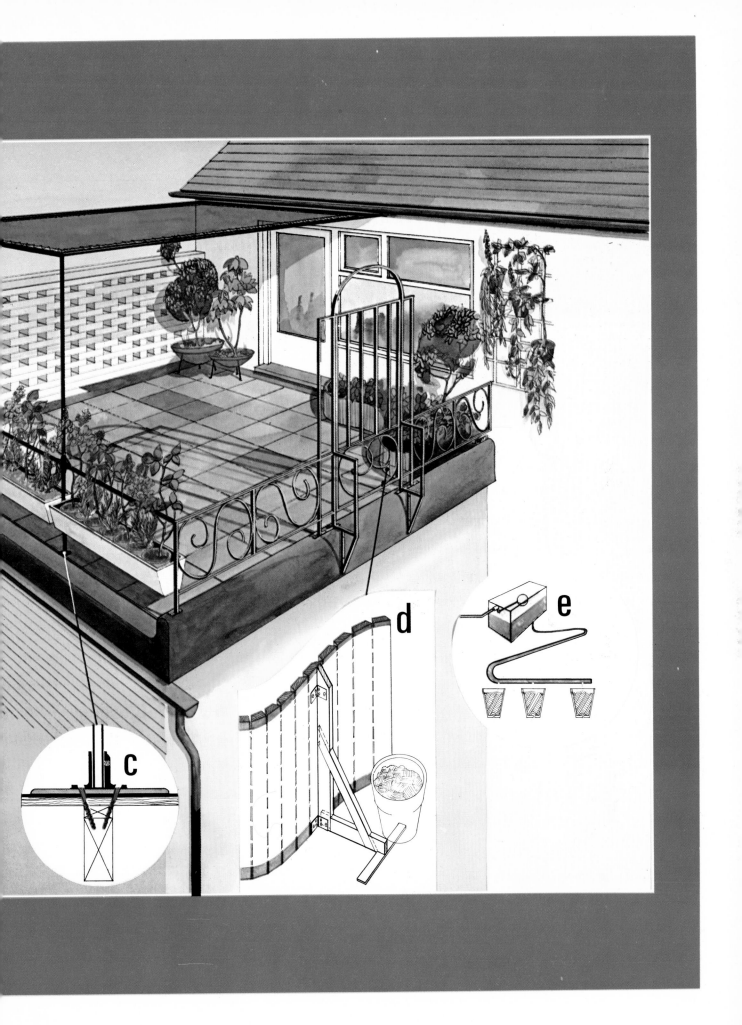

c

d

e

directly on the roof surface, contained on the outer edge by the parapet wall, and on the inside by timber shuttering, brickwork, or by a peat wall. The latter is most effective, both visually and practically, because peat holds moisture. But the planting of a flower bed directly on a roof surface is rarely done because of the vast amount of soil required. Not only does this add to the cost but, because of the additional weight, it will often necessitate strengthening the roof structure. If, however, these are not relevant considerations, laying the soil directly on the surface will enable you to have a lawn and to create effects which would otherwise be impossible with container planting.

Watering

Because of the shallow depth of the soil,

Above. The soil can be placed in raised containers so that you can garden without bending down. At the same time the troughs and stands make an attractive 'wall'. The stands could be boarded in if required.

watering is sometimes necessary twice a day under hot and sunny conditions. This of course entails a great deal of work, and when you are absent for long periods you will have to arrange for someone to water the soil in your absence. For this reason most roof gardens have automatic watering systems fitted. There are two main types of automatic watering systems, one based on direct feed, and the other on capillary feed.

In the direct feed system, a length of hose, perforated at intervals, is laid over the soil. This is

Inset left. A very ordinary roof that has been transformed with a little paint and a few plants in containers. A little effort has been well rewarded.
Inset right. A roof garden shed.

connected to a water tank which is, in turn connected to the main water supply. The water filling the tank is regulated by a ball float in the same way as an ordinary cistern. When the tank is full the float is activated and releases a quantity of water down the hose. If you are planting in containers, the hose will have to be clipped with a properly located perforation over the top of each one.

The other system uses capillary action to supply water to the roots of plants. The containers are placed in a bed of sand, and a glass

BILL McLAUGHLIN

PAUL KEMBLE

*bove. A stunning roof garden in two
ctions linked by a balcony. A lattice
reen supports climbing plants and hides
ly pipes. The containers are fenced in
ith tongued-and-grooved boarding.*

*Inset. A wooden combined garden seat and
planter. The framework is constructed from
2in. x 2in. timbers panelled in with the
same boarding as for the fence. The seat is
made from 1in. thick planking.*

re wick is placed in the container soil, running
rough a hole in the bottom and linking with
e sand. The sand is kept moist by means of
other glass fibre wick running through the
nd bed at one end, and placed in a cistern or
icket of water at the other end. The water
pply must be located at a higher point than the
nd.

hoice of plants

As space is usually limited, vertical growth
ust be encouraged. Walls and parapets can be
concealed by leading climbing plants up their
surfaces; some of the climbers could be allowed
to grow rampant and spill over the top and down
the sides of the building. If you have a really
large roof, try the Russian vine Polygonum
baldschuanicum, which is a prolific grower and
will cover vast areas. For the smaller garden, the
cup and saucer flower Cobea scandens, ivy, or
passion flowers will cover walls or fences well.

Where containers are used, there is no reason
to use one type of soil exclusively. You can grow
acid-loving plants like rhododendrons, azaleas,
camelias, fuschias, heathers and conifers in one
container, and place these alongside lime-
loving plants like pinks and clematis in another
container.

Winter flowering heathers, conifers, berried
and variegated shrubs, can provide colour and
interest when the weather is at its worst, and
many of the beds or containers can be under-
planted with spring-flowering bulbs which are
frequently earlier in shooting and flowering than
plants at ground level. Alpine plants, preferably
grown together in special containers, are
particularly suitable for roof gardens. A sink
garden of alpine flowers can provide an
attractive focal point.

Roses, incidentally, will grow just as well on a
roof as they do at ground level provided the soil
is at least 18in. or 450mm deep.

45

:dgings for paths

e problem of designing the best type
edging between a flower plot and the
wn or paving that abuts it, is one that
nfronts every serious gardener as the
out and design of the garden is
nned. To find the particular edging
at complements and blends in with the
lours and terrain of the garden, and
at the same time allows for practical
requirements such as mowing, it is best
that you are familiar with as many
different sorts as possible The problem
here, in fact, is not the realization of your
choice, as this is generally quite
straightforward and calls for only fairly
basic DIY competence, but the selec-
tion, in the first place, from the many
different styles available.

While some of the simpler forms of edging are
just as much visual demarcations between the
flower bed and the turfed or paved area that
adjoins it, as aids to keeping the lawn or path
free from stray soil or leaves, the more elaborate
borders have a decorative impact in their own
right. A narrow 'mowing strip' of concrete—
which may of course be mixed with marble chips
or small pebbles—or a run of hardwood boards,
set into the earth and supported by pegs along
their lengths, are examples of the first sort,
making first of all for neatness rather than
decoration. On the other hand, a built-up wall of
freestone or sandstone, or even suitably textured
and tinted bricks, is the type of border that earns
its place in a garden scheme for reasons over
and above its purely functional contributions.
By varying the heights of these 'walls' from one
bed to the other, you can stagger the levels of the
soil, and therefore the flowers (or whatever), in
the beds, across the garden layout.

Another factor which should be taken into

1

2

*eft. The type of edging to be used depends
the dimensions of the garden and the effect
quired. In a large area, formal hedges not
ly define the flower beds but can add a new
d intimate character to the whole garden.*

Fig. 1. *Bricks and stone blocks, discreet
or decorative, are easy to lay and well suited
to some types of plot.* **Fig. 2.** *Tree trunk
edging can be used for most borders and gives
the plot a natural and informal look.*

Fig. 3. *Wrought iron, in its many different
patterns, is itself attractive and, for plots
of large plants in particular, forms a neat
boundary without obstructing the lower parts
of the plants from view.*

3

consideration in selecting the most appropriate form of edging is the particular cultivation contained by the plot. For large plants and shrubs, for example bars of wrought iron in a pattern like that shown on page 51 serve to keep a neat appearance while not blocking out the lower sections of the plants from view.

Mowing strips

The most simple artificial border, used to mark off a garden flower plot from a stretch of lawn or pavement, is the concrete 'mowing strip'. By setting a narrow, rectangular cross section, line of concrete, like that on page 53, to be virtually flush with the surface of the lawn, you can mow right up to the end of the grass without needing to trim the lawn edges by hand. The

one third of the total depth of the strip should be buried. If you are staggering the levels on either side of the strip, one third of the depth should be beneath the lower of the two soil levels. Naturally, the earth at the bottom of the formwork should be well compacted before the concrete is laid, and a wider mowing strip, which is often used in conjunction with edging like a freestone block wall, should not be laid too close to a shrub or tree whose roots are liable to crack the concrete later.

For a slightly more decorative look, the strips can be coloured using oxide additives, which are included in the concrete mix: green, brown, blue, and yellow are some of the tints available, with the intensity of the colour determined by the amount of oxide added. Marble chips may

are simple functions of the size and nature wood you buy.

Block stone edging

Freestone or sandstone blocks, laid eit horizontally or vertically, can provide an attr tive complement to the colours in the garden well as more than adequately discharging usual practical roles that edging of any sort m fulfil. Stone suitable for use in the garden n be obtained either from a garden supplier's st or a local quarry—freestone and sandstone only two suggestions. But the best policy is doubtedly to do the rounds of your lo suppliers and see what is available at the pri you are willing to pay. Colour and texture also primary considerations, as this type

mowing strip also means that the edge of the lawn and the start of the loose soil in the flower bed are separated, and in fact can both be run up flush to one side or the other of the strip. This effectively prevents the exposed edge of the lawn and its underlying soil from eroding, or collapsing in places after a heavy fall of rain, and spilling out over the flower bed. As well as this, by making the strip a little deeper than usual you can take the level of the flower bed down a few inches should that blend in with the garden design.

To put in a mowing strip, all you need do is dig a small trench between the lawn and the bed if there is not sufficient room to work already, set up some thin wooden formwork—plywood which has been externally braced with pegs about every 18 inches should be quite adequate for this load—to the desired depth, and pour and trowel smooth a normal 1:2:3 (cement/sharp sand/$\frac{3}{8}$ to $\frac{3}{16}$in. washed shingle) mix into the mould thus made. In general, there should be half as much of the strip's depth below the ground level as there is above ground—that is,

also be used to good effect, and of course the flower bed side of the strip need not necessarily be laid parallel to the lawn side strip edge, but may incorporate a few gentle curves etc. to add an extra touch. Alternatively, small pebbles can be inlaid on the top surface of the strip. In this case the strips should be separately (i.e. not 'on site') cast in sections, with a layer of sand into which the pebbles are partially inserted at the bottom.

Hardwood boards as edging

Hardwood boards, preferably treated with a horticultural grade of wood preservative (i.e. one that does not contain any chemical toxic to vegetation), can make functional dividers between a path or lawn and a flower bed. The boards are set into the ground as shown in Fig.7, using pegs to brace the boards along the length of the run. The main advantages of this form of edging, besides its durability and ease of installation, are direct results of the properties of the material used—the depth of the edging, and the length and curvature of the sections used,

Fig. 4. Horizontally laid bricks can make a functional border between plot and lawn. Fig. 5. A formal brick wall is visually strong and especially suitable for raised and leafy plots. Fig. 6. Durable rather than decorative, concrete slabs form an adequate edging between lush flower bed and lawn. Fig. 7. Because of ease of installation and adaptability to the border's contours, hardboard has become a popular edging material

edging can significantly contribute to t decorative impact of the garden scheme chosen wisely.

Horizontally laid stone blocks or bricks, shown in Fig.4, make a pleasing continuation a concrete mowing strip, around a small circu plot in particular. The blocks used here obvious do not need to be very thick, and since it is be to set the slabs in sand or gravel rather than mortar, the colour should be selected so as n to clash with the material it is being laid Aesthetic considerations aside, fixing the sla in mortar too close to a tree or large shrub co

ed in the plot that is being surrounded may
ult in the roots cracking the mortar. While it is
elatively simple repair job to put this right if it
curs in the mowing strip, cracks in the stone-
rk mortar are difficult to get rid of, and are
tainly an eyesore the garden can well do
hout. If you are also putting down a mowing
p around the outside of the stonework, a
dth of something in the vicinity of six inches
ecommended—once again, the top surface of
strip should be flush enough to the lawn
el (half an inch above it, say) to allow you to
w right up to the edge of the lawn.

Larger stone blocks may also be set vertically
a bed of concrete, with about one third of each
b height buried, to act as substantial 'edges'
tween a lawn or path and a flower bed.

could be incorporated nicely here. The draw-
back here of course, is that since no mortar is used
in a dry stone wall, the very much reduced weight
of the small stone blocks may not lend sufficient
natural stability to the 'wall'. If you judge this to
be the case in your particular situation, a binding
1:3 (cement/builder's sand) mortar can be
employed—the amount, and visibility, of this
mortar being determined by your own prefer-
ences for either a 'dry stone' or a 'wall' look.

Concrete edging

Pre-cast concrete edging, either purpose-
made in sections and corners for the garden or
slabs that have been cut down to a suitable size
and shape, your DIY shop may do this, make an
effective and sturdy, if not very decorative,

texture can all be suited to fit in with the garden
scheme—perhaps a few rough sketches, to give
you an idea of how the possible variations can
combine and complement, would not be wasted.

'Tree trunk' edging

As the photograph on page 47 shows,
sections of tree trunks and branches, preferably
a little twisted and 'tree like', make a
different and informal edging for flower beds.
Much of their effect depends on the size and
character of the wood sections: for a border
between a paved area and lawn, fairly large
diameter trunks or branches are best, whereas
for edging around flower beds a rather smaller
size should be used. In both cases, the bark
should be stripped from the tree sections before

6

1:2½:5 (cement/sharp sand/¾ to 3/16 in. washed
ingle) mix should be used to bed the stones,
ut if you are using a stone border in conjunction
ith a mowing strip the 1:2:3 mix can be
mployed throughout. Since this latter mix in-
udes a finer grade of shingle, it is more ex-
ensive, and is in fact a better quality than is
ally needed for bedding the stone slabs—but
is plan of action does save you the trouble of
reparing two separate mixes. Visits to your
ocal suppliers should help you to decide which
tone to use, and naturally the specific size
nd design of your 'wall' should be tailored to
e individual requirements of your garden
yout.

This type of edging is especially suitable for
mall, built-up flower beds, with the blocks
losed up together to keep the raised level of
oil securely contained in the bed. Beds with a
umber of well developed and leafed shrubs
nd plants can also be edged off to good effect
y one of these rough-hewn borders. A variation
n this theme is a miniature dry stone wall, a
uitably scaled-down version of the walling

bordering around both lawn/path and lawn/
flower bed abutments. Ready-made concrete
edging is extremely easy to put in, and may be
used with or without a moving strip—to save the
final result from looking a little too much of a
'concrete jungle', you should perhaps try to
reduce the mowing strip's width to the minimum
possible. This will depend mainly on the type of
lawnmower you use, and the amount of
clearance between the cutting mechanism and
the physical extremities of the mower's body, so
a bit of preliminary research would be wise.

Concrete slabs may be used along similar lines
to the stone blocks described above to edge off
plots with fairly lush growth in them, or to act as
small retaining walls for built-up soil beds. By
casting your own slabs, however, you can introduce a great deal more variety and flair into the
use of concrete edging. This gives you the
chance to use a little initiative and you can
safely reduce the slab thickness in this case,
since they do not actually have to bear any load
greater than the pressure from the soil being
held back inside the bed. Size, shape, colour and

they are laid (mainly because insects can get in
under the bark and lay their eggs) and the wood
treated with a horticultural grade of wood
preservative.

The method of setting will depend on the size
of the sections being laid: larger pieces may
only need to be dug in well, but the smaller ones
may need to be braced along their lengths as
well. If the larger pieces are also to be used as
rough garden benches, a little smoothing of the
upper surface will save tears to clothes etc—
with this type of edging you really have to play
it by ear, and work out the finer details of the
installation from the on-site situation.

Photographs of other sorts of garden edging
also appear in this chapter: their installation is
simple, and they are given more as suggestions
than as constructional guides. With all forms of
edging, the important thing to keep in mind is
the preservation of both the colour balance so
necessary to a visually successful garden, and
the harmony of form which can as easily be
destroyed as complemented by the addition of
non-natural accessories.

A. G. L. HELLYER

Above. This shows a formal 17th century sunken garden at Hampton Court, London. The garden is surrounded by a raised walk or terrace. Left. Variations on a period garden, Ashridge, a garden in the Chilterns.

Design a period garden

Plays and films about English history have stimulated a strong interest in old gardens, whose main feature was their seclusion. An historical garden is composed of straight paths leading from one enclosed area to another, so that you cannot see everything at once. This creates a feeling of mystery as you walk around, and you can achieve this in your own garden by using some of the ideas given here.

Fashion, we know, tends to repeat itself, returning in time to the point from which it started, but the cycle is sometimes so slow that few, except the experts, realize just what

has happened. That is certainly the case with gardens, where pressures of space and time are increasingly forcing designers towards styles which had their origin three or even four centuries ago.

In medieval times life was hard, and opportunity for leisure brief. Gardens, if they could be afforded at all, were small and very simple. They were always walled or fenced against the outside world (which could still be a dangerous place) and beds were narrow and easily worked. They were often edged with bricks or small clipped shrubs such as box, rosemary or thyme, and they were filled largely with herbs for medicinal use and flavouring, with perhaps a few flowers for home or church.

As wealth increased and law and order became more widely established, gardens grew in size and complexity, though they tended to retain their regular, geometrical form. It was a long time before nature was seen as a friend or guide. Rather it was an enemy to be kept at bay, since it brought only chaos and destruction. Man's task was to restore the order which had been lost as a result of his original fall from grace in the Garden of Eden, and the patterned garden of the 17th century, however grandiose it might become, reflected this aim.

Advent of landscaped gardens

The inevitable revolution against these set ideas occurred in England early in the 18th century. Writers and artists began to deride the artificialities of formal gardens, the closely clipped shrubs and trees, the completely symmetrical patterns made by paths, beds and hedges, the complete absence of poetic or artistic grace. The natural countryside was suddenly seen to be beautiful, especially when a

Above. This garden in Stratford-on-Avon is a good example of Victorian bedding in a Tudor-style knot garden. Note how each of the flower beds is edged by a low hedge.

Above. Grass paths leading to a centre piece, here a stone urn holding foliage plants, divide these symmetrical beds. They are filled with herbs, roses and scented plants, and edged with lavender.

little touched up and rearranged by an artist and adorned with a few temples or romantic ruins.

So the landscape movement was born, and the classical British park as we know it today in places such as Stourhead, Stowe and Studley Royal came into existence. But it was a manner of gardening that required so much space and so much expenditure on soil moving, damming, building and planting that it could only be adopted by the wealthy. Ordinary people continued to garden much as they had done before and were encouraged to do so by a new development which was eventually to produce another revolution in garden styles.

Imported plants

Explorers were pushing out all over the world, deep into Asia and the Americas, to South Africa and the Indies, eventually to Australia, New Zealand and Japan. From every place they reported not only new peoples with strange customs, but also interesting and beautiful plants that had never been seen before.

Many of them were successfully brought home as seeds, cuttings or even as growing plants, and it became the fashionable thing to grow as many of these as possible in gardens. Princess Augusta, mother of King George III,

began to make such a collection of exotic plants in her own garden at Kew House which, with the adjoining garden of Richmond Lodge, was acquired by the nation nearly a century later to become the Royal Botanic Gardens, Kew.

At first the new plants from overseas were grown mainly in simple beds, such as those characteristic of medieval gardens and still to be seen in the 'family beds' of botanic gardens. But some were used to give greater variety of colour and form to gardens created in the landscape style.

The arrival in the early 19th century of the magnificent evergreen conifers of north-western America changed the aspect of many of these gardens, a change which some people still regret on the ground that the solid, conical shape and dark winter foliage of many of these trees is alien to the much softer aspect of the British countryside, with its mainly rounded trees which lose their leaves in winter.

Later in the 19th century the introduction of many fine rhododendrons and azaleas from Asia produced yet another controversial development in landscaping, since they made it possible to add to what had previously been mainly green garden pictures, solid masses of colour which appeared excitingly beautiful to some, and offensively vulgar to others.

Greenhouses

Some of the fine new plants from overseas were too tender to be grown outdoors all year

round, so methods of protection had to be devised for them. The earliest were simple houses with large windows on at least one side, heated by open braziers or flues concealed in the walls or floor.

They were known as orangeries since it was principally orange bushes that were grown in them, planted in large tubs so that they could be carried out of doors in summer for the decoration of the garden. Later the development of lighter weight rolled glass made it possible to glaze the roof as well as some of the sides, and still later the manufacture of cast iron pipes and consequent adoption of hot water heating resulted in the efficient, fully glazed and adequately warmed greenhouses which we know today.

Such greenhouses were already becoming common when Queen Victoria came to the throne, and because they made it possible to propagate exotic plants on a scale never dreamt before they produced another notable change in garden fashions. Many of these plants, though requiring protection in winter, could be grown out of doors with complete safety in summer.

So the Victorians invented 'bedding out', i.e. the practice of planting out thousands of exotic plants directly it was safe to do so and either discarding them in the autumn, to be replaced by a new batch the following year. or returning them to the greenhouse for the winter. Usually this bedding out was done in elaborate patterns in beds of geometric shape, a return to the 17th century style of gardening, though with very different plants. Therefore the effect was totally different, being much more fussy and highly coloured.

Bedding out is still the mainstay of many public parks and publicly owned open spaces,

in which several changes of plant may be made annually to maintain the brightest possible display for the longest possible period. But the outlay in money and time is too great for most private garden owners today who, if they practise bedding out at all, use it mainly to brighten up beds planted largely with hardier and more permanent things such as shrubs and herbaceous perennials.

Development of hybrids

The great influx of new species encouraged breeding, so that soon man-made hybrids became of greater importance to gardeners than the wild plants from which they had been developed. Nowhere is this more apparent than in the rose, which in medieval times had few varieties and little range in colour and form

The biggest breakthrough here has occurred during the last 100 years, with the development of entirely new races of rose, such as the Hybrid Teas, the Floribundas and the large-flowered climbers, all flowering more or less continuously from June to October instead of only once each summer in the manner of most wild and old fashioned roses. Today roses have largely taken the place of half-hardy bedding plants as a means of keeping gardens colourful for a long period, for unlike bedding plants they do not have to be replaced annually or housed during the winter in expensive glasshouses.

But the modern rose, with its requirement for annual hard pruning, is a much more formal

Above. This garden was made to the maxims of Gertrude Jekyll, the famous Victorian gardener. These are formal design with informal planting and careful use of colour.

plant than the old fashioned rose with its more shrub-like habit. These new roses look best massed in beds, yet another reason for the adoption of more formal styles of design similar to those of several centuries ago.

Later developments

Other things have tended in the same direction. As land has become increasingly expensive, gardens have inevitably become smaller and smaller. It is difficult to create effective pictures, such as those evoked by the 18th and 19th century landscapes, in gardens that measure only a few yards in each direction, but it is very easy to fill them with pleasing patterns, which is precisely what the early gardeners did. Moreover, because houses and gardens are so closely packed together, they tend to be overlooked and so greater privacy is sought by enclosure within walls, screens or hedges. Again the comparison with early styles is obvious, though now it is protection from prying eyes rather than from thieves and wild animals that is sought.

Other features have been borrowed from the past and also from different cultures. Travellers to Spain and the countries of North Africa have seen and admired the paved patio gardens made

there and have returned eager to apply similar ideas to British gardens. Unlike grass, paving requires no maintenance and will stand any amount of hard wear. It is ideal for a tiny garden that is frequently used and it can be made interesting by being laid in patterns with a diversity of materials providing different textures. Paths and paving are dealt with more fully in the following chapter, Paths and Drives.

Water too, a feature of great importance in southern gardens, can now be used easily and cheaply thanks to the introduction of long-life plastic sheets to line pools, and waterproof electric pumps which can be fully submerged to operate fountains, cascades and other water features by recirculation of the water at minimal running cost. Water gardens are dealt with fully in the chapter of that name.

This does not mean that modern gardens are being made in close imitation of either 17th century or Moorish gardens, but simply that designers are borrowing many ideas from them and freely adapting them to 20th century needs. The greatest difference of all is to be seen in the planting of these new gardens, and here the inspiration comes very largely from a half-

forgotten Victorian lady, Miss Gertrude Jekyll.

She was a gifted artist whose failing eyesight in later life made her turn increasingly to gardening. In a long collaboration with the architect, Sir Edwin Lutyens, she developed a style of planting which has dominated British gardening ever since. The late Victoria Sackville West, who at Sissinghurst Castle in kent made brilliant use of the Jekyll method, once described this as the 'maximum formality in design with the maximum informality in planting'.

Put another way, one can think of the underlying pattern of a Jekyll garden, the architectural features of which were usually contributed by Lutyens, as the skeleton of a beautiful body and the planting as the flesh which gives that beauty reality. In a garden of this kind there is never any sense of confusion, since the firm underlying pattern gives it unity and purpose. But equally there is no danger of the pattern's becoming boring since it is thickly overlaid with plants which constantly change in colour, texture and form as the seasons pass.

Miss Jekyll cared about colour more passionately than any gardener has done before, and

Above. This garden at Bowood, Wiltshir is a typical example of an 18th century landscaped garden. It is complete with a romantic folly—here a temple—and a lake

wrote about it more clearly and persuasi than anyone has done since. She also lo plants for their own sake, admiring then individuals, so that her gardens reflect all influences of the previous centuries. They patterned in a way that would satisfy any century designer; though mostly on a s scale they are sufficiently pictorial to deligh 18th century landscape gardener, and they cope with any of the rich plant material whic fascinated the 19th century collectors.

If a garden is so tiny that it cannot contain large plants, that variety can just as easily supplied with miniatures from the mount and rocky places—another widening of ga horizons which originated with the m maligned Victorians.

If you take a few hints from the gardens of historical period and apply them to your c you can quite easily create a genuine garden on practically any plot.

Above. *Artificial paving slabs form a smart path between two borders. The hard edges on each side are softened by an infill of large pebbles, and the flower beds are retained by curved concrete edging strips.*

Paths and drives

Paths, paved areas and drives provide an important part of the landscape around your house—a part that is often neglected. You can completely transform the look of your garden by constructing suitable paths and paved areas which are both functional and attractive.

You may have been so preoccupied with making alterations to your house since you moved into it that you have neglected the garden. Although it is important to keep it free from weeds and generally looking smart, its appearance can be greatly improved by the addition of a winding path, a sweeping drive, a terrace, or

just a small paved area where you can sit in the shade.

When you come to plan your path or paved area, give the matter plenty of careful thought before you get down to the job. The construction and design of paths in a garden often leads to a disappointing effect, and in some cases the garden layout can be completely spoilt.

One of the most common mistakes made is that paths are laid out in uninteresting straight lines, and often there are far too many of them. A long narrow garden will look even narrower if it is divided along its length by several straight paths.

Right. An asphalt path surrounded by well filled flower beds can give an informal appearance to an entrance drive. White chippings added to black asphalt produce a softer colour. *Right below.* You can cast your own concrete slabs in practically any shape and set them in a lawn. Here, round paving slabs in a variety of sizes provide an attractive path across a garden.

The main function of a path is to link up the dominant features in a garden as much as possible. The choice of material, whether it is coloured or of various shapes, will do much to provide interest and design in the layout of a garden. Path making is an operation which should be planned on paper beforehand, so that the best design can be made and quantities of materials can be estimated accurately.

Before deciding on the actual layout of a path, you should consider the time and amount of money you have available. Your garden may be a new one, where paths are to be laid down for the first time, or an existing garden which is to be redesigned. If you want a cottage garden effect, a formal pattern will naturally be unsuitable.

If the ground is very uneven, you may want to match paths with steps and terraces. In a small garden, the boldness of a length of path can be reduced or avoided if stepping stones are used, or if the monotony of the path is broken up by means of patterns or different materials.

Before you plan your path or paved area, consider what materials are available, and choose those that suit your particular garden.

Concrete

Concrete paths need not look harsh and plain if you give them one of the many interesting finishes available. You can apply a surface texture or add a coloured pigment to the concrete while you are laying or mixing it. You can also create the appearance of paving slabs or concrete paving by pointing in with a trowel.

Don't think that concrete slabs have to be square; it is quite easy to cast your own slabs in practically any shape—round, oblong, or hexagonal and you can lay whole paths with either straight or uneven edges. The range of possibilities for using concrete, is something that you can experiment with for yourself if you choose textures and colours carefully while blending the different effects of concrete blocks with concrete slabs. It is necessary to repair surface damage immediately.

Many gardeners mix concrete themselves using the basic ingredients of cement, sand and shingle or ballast. Some firms supply bags which contain all the necessary ingredients ready mixed, and all you need to do is to tip the contents out, add water carefully and mix thoroughly. This is an expensive way of using concrete for large amounts of work, but ideal for small jobs and for repairs. For instance, the settling cracks which appear in concrete shortly after it is laid need to be filled at once and there are always minor resurfacing jobs to be done.

Paving stones

Paving slabs can be of either natural or artificial stone, and there are many available to suit all types of garden. Stone paving is the most popular type of paving material, and can be used in a multitude of ways.

Apart from the conventional, regular arrangement on paths and patios, flagstones can be used in more formal ways to great effect. If you need a path running across your lawn, but do not want to break up the line of the grass too much, you can lay a stepping-stone path, setting the slabs slightly below the surface so as not to snarl up a lawnmower.

In a garden which is on various levels, it is often more practical to construct steps than to leave grass slopes which are awkward to mow. Paving stones make excellent steps, and you can choose the same stone in different sizes to give a more uniform appearance to a large garden on many different levels.

You can easily create a sitting-out area close to your house or under a shady tree using artificial paving slabs. Choose a colour which blends well with its surroundings—if near the house, try to match or tone the stone slabs with the bricks.

If you want a cool sitting-out area under tree, you can pave it with pale coloured slab and put a garden seat on it. For example an octagonal garden seat or bench which can be built around a tree trunk would be mos suitable.

The area round a greenhouse or kitche garden should be paved for easy, dry access all weathers. Paving slabs would be most usef here, and can be stepped gradually on slopin ground.

Using a variety of different colours creates softer effect on a patio or path, and paving slab can also be used combined with other materials such as bricks or large pebbles. This gives a les harsh appearance than a large expanse of plai

stone. However decisions about stone and tile paving depend on your requirements.

Crazy paving

Another popular paving material is crazy paving, which is available as York stone, broken paving stone, slate, and many other materials. York stone is the best type to use because of its hard wearing qualities, and is generally available in slabs 1½ and 2in. thick.

The irregular outline of crazy paving breaks up the monotony of the plain surface of a path, and it is particularly suitable for a cottage or old-fashioned garden.

If you are laying a path with crazy paving, start with the largest stones, then fill in with smaller ones. You can either lay the pieces in a concrete screed, or bed it in sand or soil. If you fill the gaps with soil, you can insert low growing plants between the slabs to produce an informal effect. Cutting and laying crazy paving needs some planning beforehand.

Brick paving

Bricks make a very attractive flooring for a patio, and are most effective on garden paths. If you buy smart new bricks you can create a smooth path, or old mellow bricks with uneven edges will give a more rustic appearance.

Special paving bricks are available, and these are more suitable than building bricks, as they are harder and thinner. Bricks naturally take longer to lay than paving slabs, but many people find them preferable in a garden because they look less harsh.

You can vary the pattern to suit the mood of your garden—a regular or herringbone arrangement will suit formal surroundings, whereas a random layout blends in better with an old-fashioned garden. As with other forms of paving, you can leave gaps in between bricks to allow plants to grow, so as to soften the effect further.

On a narrow garden path with raised beds on each side, it is often wiser to use a regular pattern. On a larger area, however, a more elaborate design would be effective. You can combine half bricks with whole bricks to make interesting patterns, and by mixing different coloured old bricks the effects will be softer. Once again, some planning on paper will help you to avoid major errors in construction.

Gravel

Gravel is a popular material for drives and narrow, little-used paths, and is the cheapest and easiest form of path to lay. The main disadvantages of gravel are that the larger forms, such as shingle and pebbles, are difficult to walk on, and small gravel is easily carried into the house.

The ground should be excavated and coping flags or bricks inserted to hold back the surrounding soil. First lay a bed of hardcore 3 or 4in. deep, and compress it by tamping and rolling. Then pour on the gravel to a convenient depth, leaving the copings just proud of the surface, and roll the gravel firmly.

You should keep gravel paths and drives clean by watering them regularly with weed killer. Remove fallen leaves with a leaf rake, and roll the surface regularly.

*ove. Bricks are easy to lay for curved *hs in an informal garden, as here, where skirt a bed at the foot of a tree. nts have been inserted between the bricks.*

Below. *A crazy paving path looks more interesting if different coloured stones are used. Here, a retaining wall built with bricks echoes the same colours used in the path.*

Tarmac and asphalt

A common covering for drives and paths is tarmacadam or asphalt, which is easier to maintain than gravel, but does not blend in so well with the surrounding garden. Its main advantage is that it will last for years if the job is done well in the first place.

You can now buy tarmac in different colours: green, red and brown as well as black; and a mottled effect can be produced by the addition of white chippings embedded in it.

The greater care you take in laying the drive the longer lasting it will be but the repair techniques for this type of drive are quite easy to master.

Plants

Don't be disappointed after constructing a path or drive by its bare, stark appearance. The addition of a few well-chosen plants will soften its outlines and help it blend in with the landscape.

There are many low-growing plants which can be planted in the crevices between paving stones, and some of these actually thrive on being trodden on. If you want to keep your path clear but soften its outline, you can grow edging plants along it.

Paving and paved areas often have crevices and planting pockets in which paving plants can be sown. The plants serve to relieve the monotony of large areas of paving, and many of them can not only be trodden underfoot without damage, but actually seem to thrive on this treatment.

Among those plants which act as a 'carpet'

Above. The path leading to a front door can take on focal interest if you pave it with a variety of coloured slabs.
Below. Three more ideas for a front path. You can cast your own crazy paving and set them in a lawn (just below the surface) or make a formal path. Opposite. Paved walks at Sissinghurst Castle.

are herbs such as mint and thyme, which give off a pleasant scent when trodden underfoot. Plants with grey or silver foliage always in well with stone or brick paths. *Frank thymifolia* has grey-green leaves with tiny star-shaped flowers, and *Potentilla alb* more rampant plant, has grey-green which spread rapidly.

Creeping Jenny (*Lysimachia nummula* with its masses of buttercup-yellow flow does equally well in full sun or partial sh Certain members of the *Arenaria* family, suc *Arenaria balearica, Arenaria purpurescens Arenaria caespitosa,* make attractive plants small crevices and the gaps between pa slabs.

Some prostrate shrubs can be used on l areas of paving, particularly *Cotonea horizontalis* and *Cotoneaster salicifolius, Carpeter dammeri* moulds itself to the cont of any surface on which it is growing.

Edging plants soften the outlines of a path large area of paving without spoiling the loc the stone. Suitable varieties include Alyss Lobelia, Candytuft, Dwarf Nasturtiums French Marigolds.

Ask your nurseryman for suitable pla depending on the kind of path and the e you want to create, and you will find your pa areas blend in better with the surroun landscape.

Take a long look at your garden and try work out how you could improve on proportions and usefulness by the addition path, paved area or flight of steps using ideas given here.

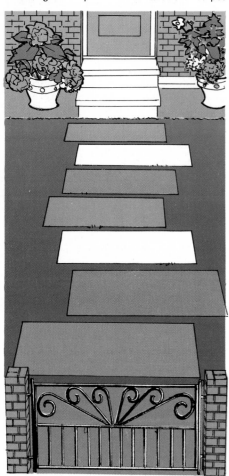

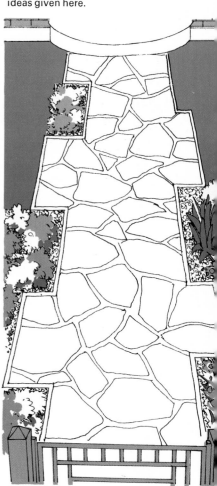